THE
FABRIC
OF
PARADISE

SCORPION PUBLISHING LTD

THE FABRIC OF PARADISE

LEONARD HARROW

WITH STRUCTURAL ANALYSIS BY JACK FRANSES

FIRST PUBLISHED IN 1988 BY
SCORPION PUBLISHING LTD
VICTORIA HOUSE, VICTORIA ROAD
BUCKHURST HILL, ESSEX IG9 5ES
ENGLAND

ISBN 0 905906 67 5

ART DIRECTION AND DESIGN · COLIN LARKIN
HOUSE EDITOR AND RESEARCH · JOHN ORLEY
PRODUCTION ASSISTANT · SUSAN PIPE
PHOTOGRAPHY · RICHARD DAVIS
MARKETING · ALAN BALL

ALL COLOUR AND MONOCHROME PLATES ARE
© SCORPION GROUP/SCOPHA

TYPESET IN LINOTYPE BERKELEY OLD STYLE BOOK
11 POINT ON 13
PRINTED ON PARILUX MATT 150 GSM
PRINTED AND BOUND IN ENGLAND BY
JOLLY AND BARBER LTD

CONTENTS

ACKNOWLEDGEMENTS

The contents of this work are primarily indebted to the late Antony Hutt, whose enthusiasm and perspicacity are its source. His early death has been a great loss not only to all his friends but to the study of Islamic art in particular.

We are also deeply grateful, as on previous occasions, to Jack Franses for the benefit of his experience in the technical analyses and for his ever-ready enthusiasm and assistance. John Orley, who assisted at every stage, also has our sincere thanks.

We gratefully acknowledge the use of the following photographs:

Antony Hutt – pp. 14, 18, 19, 22, 26, 28, 47, 89, 91, 92, 94; John Orley – p. 33; Warwick Ball – p. 32.

The reproductions of the engravings are taken from Lane, E, *The Arabian Nights Entertainments*, 1838-40.

We also acknowledge kind permission to use quoted matter from:

The Life and Good Times of William Randolph Hearst, Without Drums and *The Inheritors* G P Putnam and Sons; *The Great Pierpont Morgan* Harper and Bros.

NOTE

In the spelling of foreign words in this volume we have tried to be consistent and close to accepted transliteration systems. However, many words now common in English, which might be regarded as far from accurate by purists, have been left in their familiar forms.

LIST OF PLATES

Part of the arcade in the madrasa attached to the Royal Mosque, Isfahan, Persia, 17th century.

INTRODUCTION

THE oriental rug has been a prized item throughout its many centuries of existence, both in the regions where it has been created by hand – manufactured in a literal sense – and in the West where it has been regularly imported and also acquired as gift and tribute. It is the aim of this work that the rugs and carpets associated with it will help to bring to the notice of a wide public the proper value of these items.

It is hoped that not only their immediate beauty, but also the patient tradition which has been responsible for their creation is appreciated. The value of the rare and magnificent items with which we are dealing is now enhanced by their scarcity and by the fact that the attitudes of mind and proper discipline which were required are rapidly disappearing in the Middle East. Such pieces can now no longer be created.

However, in addition to the skill and the vast amount of labour in terms of time that the tying of the millions of knots involves, the items of the highest levels are lifted by the genius of their creators above the craft tradition to be works of art. This needs a wider appreciation of the art form and an understanding of the milieu that was responsible for it.

We regard the historical perspective as of great importance. Understanding is best increased by a knowledge of the conditions in society which produced such marvellous work. There are few great problems regarding the origins or dates of the pieces shown in this book – the examples are mainly of silk and originate from north west Persia or Turkey – but we must not forget the harsh physical environment which forms the backdrop to manufactures nor the frequently difficult social and economic environment which consideration of the history of 19th century Persia and Turkey should help crystallise in the readers' minds.

As has been frequently suggested and demonstrated elsewhere the tradition of the garden in the genre is paramount. It can be seen as a dimension of religious aspiration, as that Paradise promised to the faithful or as that earthly paradise to which so many Persians and Turks aspire, be they prince or pauper, and which cannot be avoided in any acquaintance with the art of the area. It may be argued that all the rugs in this book express the paradigm encapsulated by perhaps the most famous and hackneyed Persian poetry in the English language – that of Omar Khayyam/ Fitzgerald sitting beneath his bough in the wilderness.[1] It is rather as if the historical, social and physical background form a stark contrast with the beauty, colour and harmony of these rugs which come to us as shimmering fabrics of paradise.

NOTES
1 Fitzgerald, E, *Rubáiyát of Omar Khayyám*, London, 1944, p. 46, xi
 Here with a Loaf of Bread beneath the Bough,
 A Flask of Wine, a Book of Verse – and Thou
 Beside me singing in the Wilderness –
 And Wilderness is Paradise enow.

CHAPTER ONE
A WESTERN PERSPECTIVE

As well as acquiring precious and luxury items by trade, it seems that obtaining such things by the legalised plunder of war continued to be a familiar means of acquisition. Oriental carpets were always regarded in the West as articles of great value; all the great families and the ruling groups came to include such works as part of their collections to be handed down to later generations. Much of our knowledge of early knotted items derives from studies of Renaissance and post-Renaissance painting. Indeed, many types have taken generic names from the painters in whose work they feature.[1] Some were acquired as diplomatic gifts and ordinary purchases, some came violently as the spoils of war. Thus the great Anhalt carpet, now in the Metropolitan Museum, New York, is said to have come into the possession of the Duke of Anhalt after the Turkish withdrawal from the siege of Vienna in 1683, the last serious attempt by the Ottoman Turks to extend their power into Christian Europe, the eventual riposte to the destruction of the flower of European chivalry at Nicopolis in 1396; and there are other carpets with similar provenance.[2]

It is known that oriental rugs were traded into England during the 16th century from paintings of the period and, not least, from the records of Cardinal Wolsey. The trade was, however, fairly limited. Later in the 17th century the East India Company imported Indian carpets for auction and sale in London, but apparently soon ceased because the financial return was too low.[3] Although the trade undoubtedly continued in a small way, it awaited the revival which occurred towards the end of the 18th century and into the 19th when the oriental interest of the Romantic period and the growing importance of India to the British Empire gave it such impetus.

Apart from increasing economic and political involvement, the British public's interest in the East was given stimulus by the translation of *The Thousand and One Nights* into French by Antoine Galland in the 18th century and the increasing number of travel books, many deriving from business and diplomatic relations.

The image of an exotic East was taken up as a theme by the Romantic movement and there was interest in the arts and decorative elements of Islam. Previously in the 18th century there had been the 'Divan Club' with Sir Francis Dashwood and Lady Wortley Montagu. William Beckford, author of *Vathek* (1782), had a coffer made 'in the Persian taste' and a bedroom in Turkish style.[4] Architecture began to show Eastern influences, initially in garden architecture such as mosque-style follies and Turkish tents amongst other exotic structures. Later it was seen in major buildings where the tradition of Andalusia and Islamic India had strong influence. Thus Owen Jones's study of the Alhambra has repercussions on the design of the Crystal Palace and Osler's Gallery. Such influence also affected interior tastes, and gave rise to Moorish billiard rooms, tiles, wallpapers and ceilings. By 1870 Matthew Digby Wyatt could write about 'Orientalism and European Industry': 'We work now in almost all departments of production, especially in carpets, rugs, tiles, floor-cloth, mural decoration, paper hangings, shawls and to some extent in jewellery and mosaics, in the spirit if not in the forms of Oriental art.'[5]

Great stimulus was given to interest in the Orient by a series of important exhibitions, one of the first being the Great Exhibition in London in 1851 in which Owen Jones's work played such a prominent role. Thereafter followed a series of exhibitions which likewise proved to be powerful catalysts. Among them were Paris (1878), Vienna (1891), which was the first major carpet exhibition, Munich (1910), and later but just as important considering the enormous interest which already existed in the USA, that of Chicago in 1926.

The colonial aspirations of the Western powers brought added wealth, as any nation with pretence to world leadership found it necessary to take part in the scramble for territory. Many colonial areas' natural resources were exploited to feed industry, as in Britain, which then re-exported finished goods back to the colonies and the rest of the empire. The European economic strength increased the poverty of lesser states, such as Persia and Turkey, who could not compete and who became in due course indirect colonies of the major European powers in many areas of trade. However, the majority of people in Britain, France and other European countries did not necessarily enjoy all this wealth and those oriental ornamentations and textiles which were an important embellishment of it: the Britain of Owen Jones, we must remember, was also that of Charles Dickens. The United States on the other hand exploited its own resources without recourse to empire, and the social system of the US allowed a rise of individuals to wealth, albeit dependent on a working class.

Almost a thousand years after the conquest of the Persian empire by the first Muslims, the value always attached to the carpets and rugs of the East meant that they were much sought after in this new and distant land. The early interest of the first settlers in North America is demonstrated by the many 'Turkey' carpets imported by early pioneers, effectively a general term as all items were collected at that time in Istanbul; they were used as table covers, on floors and also hung on walls; in the restored colonial town of Williamsburg there are such pieces in several of its houses. George Washington and Jefferson are known to have had eastern carpets. Such luxury items were also imported into Salem with wealthy shipowners to the fore, and Boston from 1800; southern planters imported oriental rugs with the income of their exports from plantation produce,[6] and the prosperity of the post-Civil War period stimulated further demand.

America's interest in oriental rugs and acquisition of them by its new wealthy at the turn of the century was one of the most important factors in preserving the finest examples, and even played a major part in bolstering demand from the late 19th century onwards and helping maintain the manufacturing base.

It was the great fortunes of America which now overtook the aristocracy of Europe by creating the great collections. Those involved feature many of the great names among the so-called 'robber barons', who although their fortunes had at times been made by exploitative and hard methods proved also to be among the greatest philanthropists the world has ever seen. By this means much of the wealth that they created was led by various gifts and other channels back into the public domain. This is especially so with many of the great museum collections of the United States. The collections of the great American families almost invariably included rugs from the East.

A prominent collector of eastern art was J Pierpont Morgan. His early house in New York contained fine oriental rugs:

'. . . in its elongated, highceilinged, heavily curtained drawing room there were amply upholstered chairs, a sofa with a fringe hanging down the front, and sundry small tables of maximum inutility and instability: there were fine rugs superimposed upon a flowered carpet; every horizontal surface – mantels, tables, shelves – carried its freight of ornaments and knickknacks; . . . there was hardly a foot of wall space not covered with pictures elaborately framed in gold . . .'[7]

Pierpont Morgan was a great collector in general, although he avoided some of the excesses of his contemporaries who imported castles in sections from Europe. He was also a great traveller with a taste for the past who had little time for contemporary art and artists. He had 'a genuine affection and hunger for the rarest and finest and most beautiful achievements in the arts.'[8]

William Randolph Hearst collected everything. Although oriental rugs did not form one of his major collections he had a superb collection of them as well as one of Navajo rugs. He was thought to be a little in awe of rugs, as dealers would see him admiring them quietly with a strange reluctance to walk on them. In 1937 he decided to stop collecting and sell. He seemed less interested in money than in building everything from magazines to hotels.[9]

Peter A B Widener was also a great collector and had marvellous oriental rugs at the house at Lynnewood Hall. His grandson recalls: 'We were never allowed to touch them or any of the things in the galleries. In some cases we were not allowed to walk on the priceless rugs, spread like minted gold across the gallery floors.'[10]

John Singer Sargent painted portraits of the family but tended to be sidetracked by the beauty of the carpets and spent much time transferring the rug designs to long rolls of wrapping paper.[11]

The names of the great American families that have had fine oriental rugs in their collections would make a very long list. Apart from the Yerkes, Duponts, Chryslers, Mellons, Fortunes, Astors, Hills, Vanderbilts, Goulds, Fields, Drexels, Phipps, Fricks, and many others, there was also the widow of Horace Dodge, whose 'cottage' ($1,800,000 in 1926) was lavishly furnished and had on the living room floor a rug valued at half a million dollars.

Another exceptional individual carpet belonged to Edith Rockefeller, an avid collector. She obtained one of the so-called 'Emperor's' carpets, which had belonged to the Hapsburgs and which a bankrupt Austrian state sold after the First World War. One of a pair, the other remains in a Viennese museum.

'In the huge reception hall, called the Empire Room, she entertained such personages as Queen Marie of Rumania in 1926, and Prince William of Sweden in the following year. Royalty walked in this room on the Emperor's carpet, a rug which cost $125,000, had been made in Persia six hundred years before and had once been the property of Peter the Great.'[12]

This is the great carpet that was finally to end up in the Metropolitan Museum.

Thus the great families of America took over the historic role of the Europeans in preserving the greatest examples of the art of the knot.

The interest of collectors helped give birth to a generation of famous dealers. Among early dealers was Charles B Fritz, who worked for Cunningham and Co. of London. After the company was dissolved he bought and sold rugs profitably. In 1886 Fritz joined with La Rue who offered capital expansion and he set up in Philadelphia and then New York in 1900. He made regular trips to Istanbul, which was the main source for buyers.

Mihran Karagheusian came to the US in 1896 from Istanbul. With considerable capital he was able to import from Turkey, Persia and India. He also set up his own manufactories in the East and employed as many as 1500 people. He introduced a 'Gulistan Carpet' in 1928 with great success.

Many dealers arrived in the first years of the century. Family businesses flourished with names such as Atiyeh, Castelli, Avanozian, Topalian, Telfeyan.

Buying trips to the producing countries were helped by the family networks in the East.

Individual dealers included Gulbenkian, Kazan, and Kazanjian, amongst others, around the time of the First World War. Many high quality pieces were imported. Department stores began to allocate areas to oriental rugs and then specialist shops grew up to meet the demand, as well as itinerant sellers.

Some specialists were commissioned to select pieces for very wealthy clients. We may mention among such specialists Benguiat, Costikyan and Michaelyan.[13]

As well as Europe and the United States the worldwide appeal of the oriental rug is also felt in the Far East. Not only has Japan sought fine items currently and for many years, but there is evidence from a very early date of the Japanese interest in the art of the Middle East as regards its textiles and fabrics; an important indicator of this can be seen from the contents of the imperial Shosoin treasure at Naga, the relevant contents of which were stored away in the 8th century.

The current wealth of Japan has been attracted by quality rugs. Today new orders go to Turkish ateliers, for example, at Hereke and the Sümerbank factory. Japanese tourists also purchase rugs in the producing countries and it seems that the Japanese are now amongst the most important of buyers.[14] Current interest may be gauged by the number of lecture tours given by Western authorities on the subject and by the publication of books and catalogues.

NOTES

1 See *The Eastern Carpet in the Western World*, exhibition catalogue, Hayward Gallery, London, 1983, and articles by J Mills in *Hali*, especially vol. 1, no. 4, 1978, and vol. 3, no. 4, 1981.
2 See Bennett, I, *Rugs and Carpets of the World*, London, reprinted 1985, pp. 49, 53.
3 *The Eastern Carpet in the Western World*, pp. 25-26.
4 Darby, M, *The Islamic Perspective*, London, 1983, p. 11.
5 From *MacMillan's Magazine*, 126, April, 1870, quoted in Darby, op. cit., p. 102.
6 See Topalian, M F, 'Rug Merchants in America', *Hali*, June, 1982, no. 16, p. 361.
7 Allen, F L, *The Great Pierpont Morgan*, New York, 1949, p. 40.
8 Cited in ibid., p. 146; from Mitchell, E P, *Memoirs of an Editor*, 1924.
9 Tebbel, J, *The Life and Good Times of William Randolph Hearst*, London, 1953, p. 308.
10 Widener, P A B, *Without Drums*, New York, 1940, p. 50.
11 Widener, op. cit., p. 71.
12 Tebbel, J, *The Inheritors*, New York, 1962, p. 220.
13 Topalian, op. cit., p. 362.
14 Information supplied by John Orley from interviews conducted in Turkey in 1987.

Mahan, Persia. The idyllic setting of the Shrine of Shaykh Ni'matallah.

CHAPTER TWO
THE RUG IN THE EAST

THE rug is an intrinsic part of the lifestyle of the Islamic world. It is used in many walks of life, from tent to palace, and is a frequent and perhaps only furnishing, being used to sleep, eat and sit on; the warmth and softness provide comfort, and the colour and design a decoration; many are used for prayer, perhaps as an aid to meditation, and for many families the best examples are a repository of wealth.

Rugs are usually divided into two main classes: those described as 'tribal' and those productions which are created in an urban environment. Tribal work is often coarse and unsophisticated in technique. As well as pile rugs many flatweaves are produced. Knotting by hand is the preserve of the womenfolk and the work created often forms part of their dowry. The importance in the household also applies to the town where the large fixed looms give greater scope for artistry and technique, where men are also involved in the knotting and design.

In past ages, and even to a great extent in the present day, it was the richer stratum of society which controlled the creation of rugs, although their involvement in the actual production was minimal. Since much emphasis was placed by the wealthy on their rugs and carpets, it was they who ordered the very best and thus stimulated creative technique. This is an important fact to note even within the Muslim world: rulers were often in the early centuries in direct control of the fine textile and, probably, rug manufactories. This was part of the royal workshop tradition (the *tiraz* tradition), which was following old Persian and Byzantine precedents.[1] The potentates of Constantinople, Baghdad and the great cities of the East not only gained revenue by controlling the trade but were also able to ensure that such excellent work was primarily available to the highest in the land so that they could be, and be seen to be, surrounded with a splendour appropriate to their station.

Under the Safavids, Mughals and Ottomans there were royal manufactories. The silk manufactory of the Ottomans at Hereke in Turkey also began producing carpets at some time after 1840[2] which in due course stimulated the great ateliers of Kumkapı in Istanbul.[3] Today in Turkey, for example, many major dealers similarly stimulate production by having their own workshops in various parts of the country. The courts and courtiers were also major patrons of the other arts and many of the elements in literature, architecture, ceramics, metalwork, the arts of the book and so on, form part of the repertoire met with in textiles and rugs. As has been mentioned, this is dominated by the use of colour and the image of the garden/paradise.

A feature of Islamic urban society was the way in which the trades and crafts had always been theoretically subjected to government control through inspectors, a control which may have had strong implications for rugs in preserving quality and interpretation. There were also organised guilds to regulate trade production and these probably extended to rug manufacturing. Town guilds strictly controlled members, standards and prices, although such controls began to break down in the 19th century under pressure of Western imports,[4] which helped preserve also artistic concepts and techniques. Their links with dervish sects, which we consider in a later chapter, remain to be fully investigated.

Government inspectors were also responsible for tax collecting and maintaining order, standards, weights and measures, as well as dispensing instant punishment to offenders.[5]

Most forms of artistic output in the area were, in fact, produced for specific patrons who were usually rulers or kings. Thus apart from any inherent merit, art had a role to fulfil as part of the accoutrements of a court. Some kinds of textiles and carpets, like other art, were often reserved exclusively for royal consumption or produced as a royal monopoly, especially silk products. As well as being an essential trading cargo of exotic goods the carpets and rugs became part of elaborate gift ceremonies, rewards for services rendered or given at special festivals, or presented as diplomatic gifts which is how many of the greatest examples of carpets (now usually in museums) are believed to have reached Europe: the great Hapsburg hunting carpets, for example, now in Vienna and the New York Metropolitan Museum of Art, are said to have once belonged to Peter the Great and were presented by him to the Hapsburgs.[6]

Hereke, near Istanbul, produced the finest textiles for the Ottoman court and delivery of new batches to the royal household was always an occasion of great excitement as the women of the harem chose the finest pieces; any left over were sent on to other royal establishments or finally sold in selected shops in the closed bazaar.[7]

Diplomatic gifts were still made, as for instance during Kaiser Wilhelm's visit to Hereke in 1898 when he received an enormous silk carpet produced on the large silk looms of the town manufactory. Some evidence also suggests that the Kumkapı ateliers were originally established, or at least stimulated, by the need to provide gifts of a diplomatic nature.[8] Indeed, many fine rugs were found stored in the Ambassador's Treasury in the Topkapı in 1924.[9]

Increasing awareness of Western economic and political exploitation of the East led to the introduction of textile machinery and workers in various regions.[10] Rulers in Turkey and Persia also wanted the technical expertise of the West, which was seen as its strength and a means to compete with it. This is clear from events at Hereke which brought in, in traditional manner, expertise from outside, from Lyon to Kirman.

As previously mentioned, the great exhibitions stimulated Western interest. In like manner, they gave the East an opportunity to see the great classical examples of its own heritage and stimulated them in turn, although both Persian and Turkish taste paradoxically was often for French art nouveau.[11]

Today much rug manufacture is for export and even tourism. Women and young people are frequently employed on a full or part-time basis. Often there is a cottage industry of outworkers, organised by dealers who collect the finished work; currently this may mean a rug is not woven in the area attributed to its traditional form, a feature increasing with the improvement of modern communications.[12] Although work of very high quality is rarely available, modern production in the traditional areas suffers because of the pressures of the profit motive, the pace of demand and changes in fashion. The changes in aspirations of traditional manufacturing communities as a result of Western influences are eroding the tradition of centuries for ever.

The confusion has been made worse by conflict in the Middle East. The war between Iraq and Iran has adversely affected Iran's trading position. In particular, its foreign exchange rates have meant a depression at the lower end of the market. This is at a time when other areas are using the traditional Persian methods and designs to establish their own manufactories, with centres as distant as China and North Africa.

NOTES

1 Serjeant, R B, *Islamic Textiles*, Beirut, 1972, p. 7 et seq.
2 Beattie, M, 'Hereke', *Hali*, November, 1981, vol. 4, no. 14, p. 130.
3 Bensoussan, P, 'The Masterweavers of Istanbul', *Hali*, 1985, no. 26.
4 See 'Ḥarīr', 'Akhī' and 'Ṣinf' in *The Encyclopaedia of Islam*, second edition.
5 See 'Hisba' and 'Muḥtasib', *EI²*.
6 Kendrick, A F, Pope, A U, and Thomson, W G, *The Emperor's Carpet and Two Others*, London, 1928.
7 Beattie, op. cit., p. 130.
8 Miller, D, *Zareh Penyamine*, catalogue, London, n.d.
9 Beattie, op. cit., p. 129.
10 Beattie, op. cit., p. 131. See also MacFarlane, C, *Turkey and its Destiny*, London, 1850, vol. 2, pp. 620-621.
11 Beattie, op. cit., p. 131.
12 This is especially true of Hereke, where many of the rugs purchased by local dealers are knotted in other areas, people travelling from as far away as Konya to sell rugs and then purchase silk and the distinctive Hereke cartoons to carry back with them. Information supplied by John Orley from interviews conducted in Turkey in 1987.

CHAPTER THREE
THE QAJARS

FTER the death of Nadir, Persia was mainly controlled by Karim Khan Zand, based in Shiraz, until he too died in 1779 and the Qajars emerged as the most powerful grouping. These founded a dynasty which ruled the country until after the First World War.

During the classical period of carpet manufacture in Persia the great centres which retain and later even regain their reputations are those of Tabriz and the north west, the areas of Isfahan and Kashan and also Kirman in the south east. The quality and magnificence of their work is now to be seen mainly in the great museums of the world, although it would be sad to forget the conditions and difficult circumstances under which it was produced.

The Qajar monarchy in Persia followed that period of upheaval which occurred after the downfall of the Safavids, under whose rule historic Persia is generally considered to have reached its most impressive heights in terms of culture and influence. The Qajars recognised absolute power and the Shah was considered 'the Shadow of God upon Earth'.

The pomp of their court rapidly increased as is seen in paintings[1] of the period and from textiles and rugs. State officials were promoted or demoted at the whim of the Shah, but during their dynastic reign Persia, under pressure from external powers above all, as in 1858 when Nasir al-Din was coerced into setting up a cabinet of ministers, gradually made the move from a medieval society based on tribal leaders and landowners towards a constitutional monarchy modelled on Western lines. Thus the power of bureaucrats and officials increased to the disadvantage of tribal leaders and landowners.

At the beginning of Qajar rule bureaucratic positions were held within families and passed on by inheritance. However, they were not the secure, inviolable positions those in the West tend to associate with bureaucracy. Because of their access to power and wealth, bureaucratic positions were coveted and officials were frequently exiled or killed. Since support and safety could be bought, those who survived longest were those who accumulated the most wealth. The object was to establish one's fortune as quickly as possible and to display it, which in turn fuelled the covetousness of others. Thus the despotic cycle continued, producing a greater and greater level of corruption and patronage.

Later, the practice of selling offices became widespread, and so much so that officials were pocketing the taxes they should have been raising in order to pay for their original purchase of the office. Consequently the central government was starved of revenue: a process which resulted in the grave crisis that Tehran found itself in during the 1840s; this necessitated the financial reforms which proved so unpopular to the upper and middle classes. Equally the burden of tax falling on the peasants increased to compensate for loss of revenues from government offices and the provinces, further stressing the divisions between central authority and the people. The difficulties of rug manufacture during the period must have been considerable.

The tribal element proved difficult to integrate within the developing bureaucratic structure. Groups such as the Kurds, Afshars and Qashqa'is had firmly established themselves in controlling positions and supplied most of the Shah's military capability. Tribal leaders were often provincial governors and it was only gradually that those positions were relinquished to Qajar princes.

The system worked on the basis that a governor had absolute power in his area. His only duty was to provide a fixed sum of revenue and a requisite number of troops for the central government. The only check placed on governors was the vazir who was a kind of overseer responsible to the central government, although after 1862 when Persia became a link in the telegraph system between Britain and India somewhat stricter control of the provinces was established.

Often governors failed to pay any tax at all to the central government which resulted in internal armed conflicts. Rich provinces like Azarbaijan produced so

Side portal of the Royal Mosque, Qazvin, Persia, Qajar period, early 19th century.

much revenue for the governors that they were frequently tempted to rebel. This, coupled with the often bitter disputes to decide succession to the throne, led to much instability. The accumulation of wealth in this manner by governors not only produced conflict in the upper echelons of government but also antagonised the lower classes of society who were forced to contribute to the many excesses of provincial courts, a burden which resulted in frequent disturbances.

Since the army was collected and maintained in an almost feudal style by governors, tribal leaders and landowners in the name of the central government, the government had little control. Its own ability to raise men was hampered by its lack of revenue and dependence on the provinces. Consequently those troops it did raise were often underpaid, lacking in morale and disaffected. Coupled with this was the problem of the short campaigning season, always a difficulty in feudal-style societies, and the lack of modern arms. Bows and arrows, clubs and shields were still used, supplemented by long muskets and a few pieces of artillery.

This replacement of a tribal-based society by a bureaucracy was only one factor in the difficulties which Persia faced under the Qajars. Perhaps most important of all were the external pressures which were brought to bear on Persian society. Chief amongst those exerting pressure were the Western powers and, in particular, Russia and Britain. Their interference assumed decisive importance in the latter years of the Qajar dynasty.

Together with the Western powers Persia also suffered from conflict with its neighbours, notably Ottoman Turkey, until that country became itself so weakened by Western interference that it no longer had the capability to attack Persia under its own initiative.

☆   ☆   ☆

The system of authority within Persian society was divided between Shah and governors, the local police and religious officials. The Shah held the supreme authority although governors were almost autonomous within their provinces. Local police were responsible for local offences and religious law was administered by qadis and mujtahids.

In the absence of banks, merchants provided all the funds for rulers and the rest. Although of lower class origin the merchants advanced themselves and integrated with the ruling class by means of judicious marriages. One of the strongest alliances in society was that between the bazaar merchants and the religious classes, which meant that the bazaar often closed down in favour of religious protests against the government. Naturally, the interruption to trade and financial dealing exerted enormous influence upon the government.

In the cities the craft guilds proved a strong force and there were often popular outbreaks against the Shah or the various provincial governors. In the countryside the peasants provided the labour on the land and were often compulsorily recruited into the army. The relationship of guilds involving rug manufactures and associated trades, along with the emergence of societies politically active and those with strong religious affiliations remains to be investigated.

These very disparate classes were united by the concept of a Perso-Islamic culture but not always harmoniously. Due to the different modes of production and existence, cities were separate in their aspirations from the countryside and insular, which helps explain why particular styles of rug are readily associated with a particular town or area. Any weakness in central government authority often led to fear in the cities of civil disturbance and tribal raiding in the countryside. Conflicts between the government and religious classes over the use of mosques as asylum, which was frequently the only refuge for individuals from the excesses of the state, were later complicated by the use of Russian and British missions as asylum centres.

The north/south division of Persia played an important role in the social consciousness. It stemmed partly from the division of population into Turkish and Persian racial elements but was exacerbated by the interference of the Western Powers. In general, the north was favoured with prosperity and the south was prone to disorder.

Detail from spandrel in the 19th century Ibrahim Khan complex, Kirman, Persia, with figures and motifs also seen in rug design.

The natural inclination of such a society was in general extremely conservative. The cultural fabric did not readily permit the reform and change which would lead to any kind of technological advances like those being made in Western societies. In fact, the greatest unifying force for the country was its opposition to the Western powers. In the arts, including rugs and textiles, traditional values and skills seem to have only been subverted slowly to Western influence during the 19th century.

This opposition to the West had been in little evidence at the beginning of the 19th century when the prime concern had been with the Shah's despotic rule. Foreign policy was an issue which did little to raise the anger of the majority of people. There were some disturbances, as at Tehran in 1829 when a Russian envoy was killed in reaction to the treaty of Turkomanchay which ceded considerable territory to the Russians, but it was not until the more obvious encroachment of the Western powers that opposition to their machinations became more vehement and widespread. There then occurred a rapid growth of Islamic nationalism with the perception of the Shah's weakness regarding the Powers. Allied with this nationalism, the movement for liberal reform increased amongst intellectuals and the ruling classes who hoped to resist foreign domination by setting up institutions comparable with the West's.

Britain and Russia were the prime manipulators of Persian domestic policy within the 19th and early 20th centuries, although France had also staked a claim at the beginning of the 19th century. Russia's prime area of interest, because of its proximity, was northern Persia while Britain attempted to control the south because of its interest in the Indian subcontinent. The British deemed this necessary since they regarded any extension of Russian power southwards as a deliberate threat to their sphere of interest.

Russia and Britain pursued varying policies for their own ends. Britain's strategy lay in attempting to strengthen Persian central government through reform in order for Persia to resist Russia. Russia, however, was more interested in destabilising Persia in order to put pressure on Britain and ultimately to open a route through to the Gulf and Indian Ocean.

The British found their policy extremely difficult to implement. It involved a delicate balance between keeping Persia independent and keeping Persia weak. If the country became too powerful and confident in its territorial position it would naturally prove a threat to British possessions in India and the connecting trade routes. There had been clear evidence of this in the Persian attacks on Herat in Afghanistan. Equally, this position of strength might alarm the Russians who would be even more likely to launch an invasion of Persia. Such an occupation would constitute an even bigger threat to British possessions in the subcontinent. On the other hand, if Britain allowed Persia to disintegrate it would undoubtedly fall into Russian hands, either directly through military intervention or, more likely, as a puppet state. Russian policy proved difficult only in so far that its overt control of Persia might lead to a risk of all-out war with Britain.

Both powers had their own factions within Persia. The Persians mostly feared the Russian military threat in the north and British economic domination in the south. However, Britain had not been adverse to acts of force on those occasions when Persia had taken a military initiative against British possessions. In general, most Persians resented the British presence in Afghanistan.

Fath 'Ali Shah after his accession in 1797 and also his son 'Abbas Mirza recognised the need to modernize the army in order to counter the Russian threat, although it seemed impossible that this would ever be accomplished given Persia's politico-economic structure. Likewise technological change was spurred on by the military necessity. It was, in fact, the Russians, seeking to gain an internal influence, who made a decisive move to increase the efficiency of the cavalry when in 1878 they provided arms and officers to train a Cossack brigade. The British response was to renew pressure on Persia for increased trade.

Trade between Persia and Britain varied in different periods. The balance of trade with Russia swung considerably in favour of Russia after its invasion of 1826 and increased in dominance towards the end of the 19th century. The importance of Tabriz in the north west, adjacent to Russia as well as Turkey, was maintained as a manufacturing centre and entrepot for exports of rugs to the West, a situation apparently emphasised by increased demand after 1870.[2] The ability to supply demand was also affected by recovery from the silk disease, pebrine, which was rampant for much of the period in question.[3]

Much of the initial trade between Britain and Persia in the Safavid 16th and 17th centuries was conducted via India, but the ensuing period saw a considerable reduction in the volume. When the Trabzon–Tabriz route opened in 1830 trade rapidly increased again, although it never achieved its former balance. The British share of the trade grew considerably, according to the figures quoted by Curzon[4].

However, British investment in Persia remained minimal. In 1872 there were wholesale Persian concessions granted to the British Baron Reuter for railways, roads, irrigation construction and the formation of a National Bank. It was hoped that the economic involvement of Britain would encourage Britain's support for Persian independence from the threat of Russia, but ironically Russian opposition to the deal was so great that the Persian government was intimidated into reversing its decision. Nasir al-Din reached a secret agreement with the Tsar that there would be no building of railways, roads or other communication facilities without Russian permission. This agreement, unknown to the British, flew in the face of their policy to encourage trade, improved communications and government reform.

Nasir al-Din, in a desperate effort to survive, continually attempted to play the two powers off against each other. In 1888 he opened up the Karun river to navigation by all nations and in 1889 allowed Reuter to found the Imperial Bank of Persia. However, the Russians soon forced him to backtrack yet again on communications construction. The last years of Nasir al-Din were marked by corruption and neglect, a lifestyle which convinced the nationalist movement of the despotic and whimsical nature of the Shah's rule and resulted in Nasir al-Din's assassination. With the accession of his son Muzaffar there then began a wholesale carve up of Persia by the European powers.

The unrest came to a head in 1905-06 with widespread riots and protests at tyranny and corruption. Merchants likewise feared the encroachment of foreign competition. The closure of the Tehran bazaar forced the instigation of a National Consultative Assembly called the Majlis. When Muhammad 'Ali succeeded Muzaffar al-Din he repeatedly tried to rid himself of the Majlis with Russian and British connivance, even subjecting it to armed attacks in 1907 and 1908, but failed and was eventually forced into exile. The remaining Majlis, however, was severely restricted by the interference of Russia and Germany who had reached an agreement on the Persian question at Potsdam in 1910. It remained only for the First World War and its aftermath to reduce the country to a state of anarchy until Riza Khan took control in 1921 and established, very much like Mustafa Kemal in Turkey, a series of political, financial and educational reforms.

NOTES

1 Falk, S J, *Qajar Paintings*, London, 1972.
2 Edwards, C, *The Persian Carpet*, London, 1967, p. 56.
3 Beattie, op. cit., p. 131.
4 Curzon, G N, *Persia and the Persian Question*, London, 1892, vol. 1, pp. 525-528.

Mihrab detail, 14th century, Jami' Mosque, Yazd.

CHAPTER FOUR
TABRIZ AND THE NORTH WEST

TABRIZ and the north west of Persia dominate the rugs of Persian origin in this work, and its turbulent history in the 19th century makes the quality and beauty of its manufactories the more remarkable.

Tabriz has long been famous as one of the greatest producers of Persian rugs. In spite of its vulnerable position in the north west of Iran, not far from the borders of the USSR, Turkey and Iraq, a position which has subjected it to much damage by both environmental and political action as well as contributing to periods of considerable wealth, it has maintained an artistic tradition of the highest quality.

The city is situated in the province of Azarbaijan, an area of extinct volcanoes on high plateaux (Mount Sahand, for example, is 12,138 ft high and Mount Ararat, just over the border in Turkey, reaches 16,946 ft). Consequently, the climate is especially harsh in winter, the temperature sometimes dropping as low as 20 to 30 degrees centigrade below zero. The summers are warm but not especially hot and the rainfall is often heavy. It is one of the rare areas of Persia where dry farming can be practised.

Communications follow routes through the defiles and valleys or cross the high plateaux, where agriculture is confined to the rearing of sheep, goats and, especially amongst semi-nomadic tribes like the Kurds, horses. In the valleys and lower land the earth is much more fertile and the climate kinder, enabling the growth of cereals, fruit (including almonds and apricots), tobacco and cotton, two crops which have been especially important in Tabriz's history. Azarbaijan in Curzon's time was known as the 'granary' of north Persia and the city of Tabriz was surrounded by irrigated gardens and orange and red mountains.

It is this position in a fertile but difficult terrain which has contributed so much to Tabriz's importance both strategically and economically. Two major routes existed in the 19th century as arteries of trade: through Turkey to Trabzon and through the Caucasus to Russia.

Not only does Tabriz suffer from a harshness of climate but the location is also subject to frequent earthquakes. Consequently, most buildings within the city are only built of lightweight materials to one or two storeys. Curzon reports that there were at least five earthquakes between 1700 and 1900. In 1721 Krusinski recorded a death toll of 80,000 and in 1780 an estimated death toll of 40,000.[1]

Nevertheless, the area was and is heavily populated compared with the rest of Iran. There existed a mixture of peoples in the Tabriz area during the period of the creation of our rugs: not only Persians but also Kurds and Armenians. However, the majority of people in language and descent appeared Turkish. In addition, there was a considerable American and European presence, due to the mercantile and diplomatic community, which resided in the Armenian quarter near the various consulates. The population figures which Curzon quotes from his sources are 30,000 in 1810 (using Kinneir as a source) and 50,000 in 1812 (using Morier). By 1892 the population had risen to an estimated 170,000 to 200,000 people.[2]

When one considers the history of Tabriz and the surrounding area it is surprising that any strength of cultural tradition has ever persisted within the city, but it may, paradoxically, be just those vicissitudes of history which have produced Tabriz's inspiration: a constant flux of armies and invaders, of destruction and rebuilding, of peoples with different cultural backgrounds, of poverty and wealth have created a richness in spirit and expression which informs especially its silk and woollen manufactures.

During the Qajar period of Persian history, in which most of the rugs described in this book were produced, Tabriz was persistently under threat, like its neighbour Turkey, from the encroachment of the growing powers of the West, and in particular Tsarist Russia.

Aqa Muhammad, the first Qajar ruler, who had taken control of Azarbaijan after the death of Karim Khan, was frequently involved in clashes with Russian forces. Azarbaijan, being one of the most valuable of Persian provinces in terms of the wealth and manpower which it contributed, naturally exerted a great attraction for the Russians. Much of the Persian army for the Russian war in 1826 was levied in the province, 36,000 men in all, but many were un-uniformed and lacking in discipline according to Curzon.[3] Most men were called out for six months every three to four years. By the time of Curzon's writing at the end of the 19th century, a large army camp outside Tabriz housed some 8,000 to 9,000 men who were drilled by an Austrian officer.[4]

The connection with Russia not only arose from Russian designs upon the province but also from natural factors of terrain and situation. In fact, Tabriz was linked with the Russian railway system long before Persia had a restricted and rudimentary rail system of its own.

Apart from this interest of the European powers in Azarbaijan, at the beginning of the 19th century before the Ottoman Empire became weakened by internal pressures and Western machinations, the Ottomans were strong enough similarly to covet the province.

The hostilities between the powers over the province were more or less continuous during the 19th century. In 1811 war broke out with Russia after sporadic hostilities and a treaty was concluded in 1813 in which Russia agreed to help the heir apparent, 'Abbas Mirza, in his bid to secure the succession to the throne. It was the policy of the Persians to employ possible heirs as governors of provinces, with the heir apparent administering one of the wealthiest areas. However, the succession was never fully guaranteed, and military clashes frequently occurred to determine the rightful heir. Thus it served 'Abbas Mirza's purpose to have an ally as strong as Russia and it also served Russia's purpose to have such a direct influence on Persian affairs.

A brief interlude of peace then occurred before clashes with the Ottomans and humiliating defeats at the hands of the Russians (1825-28), when Tabriz was occupied.

The 1828 peace treaty of Turkomanchay enabled the Russians to extract considerable trade concessions from Persia and establish favourable conditions for foreign merchants. However, in the 1830s a trade route was opened from Tabriz to Trabzon[5] in an attempt by 'Abbas Mirza to bypass the Russians and establish stronger connections with the British. It was about this time that cloth manufacture was introduced to Tabriz by the Englishman, Armstrong.[6] Fulling mills were eventually established at Khoi and spinning, carding and weaving were carried on near Tabriz. This must have affected and possibly stimulated local rug manufacture. However, the trade deteriorated in 1838 when the Persians attacked Herat, much to the chagrin

of the British who saw Afghanistan as within their sphere of interest.

After the death of 'Abbas Mirza, the position of heir apparent fell to Muhammad Mirza, who duly set off for Azarbaijan. However, the Russians and the British, who supported Muhammad, feared the possibility of a civil war with the Shah's other sons who contended Muhammad's position. Bad administration in the last four years of 'Abbas Mirza's governorship in Azarbaijan had already led to central government bankruptcy. By the time that Muhammad Mirza had arrived in Tabriz, his unpaid and underfed army were almost mutinous. Muhammad had further difficulties, according to Curzon: in 1834 Fraser[7] noted the ordinary people's loathing for the Qajars, mostly because of the harsh rule imposed by a system in which the provinces were nominally in charge of the Shah's sons. Nevertheless, the British provided the means to win over the troops and Muhammad made a successful march on Tehran in 1834 accompanied by Russian and British envoys.

A series of conflicts with the Kurds in 1835 also ravaged the province. Further disorders occurred in Isfahan, Shiraz and other towns. In the face of these problems Muhammad was having great difficulty in levying troops in Azarbaijan due to the government's bad financial position. Moreover, bribery and corruption were rife in government offices, which had incurred an enormous number of debtors, and consequently there was no pay available for the army.

The growing schism in the Persian population as a whole became steadily more apparent. The Persians resented the Azarbaijani Turks in Muhammad's conquering army. The economic divisions of Persia aggravated the situation. North west Persia, and especially Tabriz, was much more prosperous and heavily populated than the rest of Persia, and the Azarbaijanis often received preferential treatment from the central government, since to antagonise them risked driving them into the camp of the Russians. Elsewhere, particularly in the south, the excesses of the central government were more readily apparent.

Muhammad Shah died in 1848 and was succeeded by Nasir al-Din. As Muhammad before him, Nasir al-Din, in order to assert his authority, was faced with the task of moving an unpaid army – although this time from Tabriz to Tehran. The wealthy Tabriz merchant community came to his rescue and extended a sufficient loan to act as incentive to the troops.

During Nasir's reign, Mirza Taqi Khan (entitled 'Amir Nizam') undertook several reforms. More troops were stationed in Tabriz as part of the reform of the army, and the pensions and salaries of the financial administration were withdrawn or reduced. This occasioned great resentment in Azarbaijan amongst the

An Eastern market from *The Arabian Nights*.

upper and religious classes.

Not only did the wealth of the upper classes take a fall in this respect but the finances of the mercantile community in Tabriz were severely affected by a continuing rebellion against government authority in Khurasan and further Kurdish rebellions. Caravans carrying goods were constantly raided. In addition, the harvest had failed for the third time, causing a spate of bankruptcies. As a consequence many merchants moved their operations to Tiflis in Russia. It had also been the time of those disturbances centred on Sayyid 'Ali Muhammad, known as the Bab, whose religious and political agitation had been viewed as heretical by the authorities but who nevertheless had won a considerable following throughout the country. Along with a number of followers he was eventually seized and put to death in Tabriz in 1850. The general discontent led to the murder of Amir Nizam in 1851 in Kashan Bagh-i Fin.[8]

Continued Russian interference in Tabriz added to the unsettled situation. In 1853 the Russians persuaded the Shah to prepare a military expedition at Tabriz against the Ottomans, but it came to nothing.

The disorder in Tabriz was apparently endemic and the backdrop to its rug manufacture. In 1857, threats of the people to reimpose Bahman Mirza (the former governor who had defected to the Russians) and the possibility of a Russian occupation led to the interruption of trade and soaring inflation.

From 1857 to 1900 growing discontent with the forms of government caused an undercurrent of disturbance in Tabriz. Although Curzon[9] attributed the discontent mostly to problems between the Turkish element of the population and the Persians, that is, a religious-political conflict between Sunni and Shi'i sects, and considered that the unpopularity of the Qajars had somewhat abated, there is no doubt that Tabriz had become a focus for nationalist aspirations. This was coupled with tensions produced by border disputes between Turkey and Persia in 1870, 1873 and 1874. The situation was further complicated by continued Russian political manoeuvring and intriguing designed to oust the influence of the British.

As in Turkey, the Western economic penetration of the country continued apace and served to impoverish the general population and increase the government's dependence to an even greater degree. Curzon[10] noted that despite the volume of trade going through Tabriz there were many complaints of commercial difficulties, and small profits were occasioned by long credits, rapid changes in exchange-rates and fraudulent bankruptcies. This last tactic was adopted by some unscrupulous Persian traders and aided by bribes to mullahs.

There was a resurgence in local goods in the later years of the century. This would also apply to rug production. In fact, such a view is corroborated by other sources[11] who note a revival of rug manufacturing in the late 19th century after its decline in the 18th century and this is attributed to the energy of the merchant community in Tabriz who also supplied pieces to the Qajar court. Also noted is the long tradition of production in Tabriz and the workshop which was set up in the Safavid period under Tahmasp.

Not only was the overall balance of trade weighted enormously in favour of the the Western powers, however, but concessions were given to individual foreign subjects which led to enormous unrest in the country. One such incident occurred in 1890 when a British subject, Major Gerald Talbot, was granted control of tobacco export.[12] Tabriz, along with other Persian cities, was ablaze with protest. The religious classes and merchants formed an alliance, both fearing the encroachment of Western economic power and Christian culture. The Russians, it was rumoured, had already sensed the unpopularity of the measure and fomented unrest, which quickly spread. Almost everyone in Persia did, in fact, stop smoking! The size and vehemence of the protest, which was as much directed at the weakness and corruption of the administration as at foreign intervention, was so strong that the Shah was soon forced to back down. The incident, however, seriously weakened the Shah and gave encouragement to those forces seeking government reform.

Constant interference by the Europeans and the rumbling undercurrent of discontent culminated in 1896 in the assassination of Nasir al-Din. He was succeeded by Muzaffar al- Din, in whose reign Belgian customs officials were introduced into Azarbaijan in 1899 in an attempt to tighten up the collection of revenue. It was a move strongly resented by the population and in 1905 the Belgian director was dismissed.

Tabriz had by now become the focus for the leaders of the Constitutionalist Party, amongst whose declared aims was the establishment of a parliament on Western democratic lines. The continued efforts of the Shah to suppress movements for constitutional change were aided by the British and Russians. With their help, in 1908, the Shah attacked the Majlis in an attempted coup d'état. Tabriz, a centre of support for the nationalists, was blockaded by royalist troops. Much of this base was formed by bourgeois liberals but also consisted of Persian Social Democrats. Many Tabriz residents had migrated to the Caucasus to work in the petrol industry, especially in Baku, and had returned with Marxist ideas. In 1909 the Russians, who already had some troops stationed in Tabriz, occupied the city on the pretext of allowing foodstuffs in. After the Shah's defeat, the Russians decided to act directly against the nationalists themselves. In 1911 they seized and

Detail of the stucco mihrab, Haftshuya, Persia, early 14th century.

executed nationalist leaders in the north west Persian cities of Tabriz, Rasht and Enzeli.

Matters did not improve. With the outbreak of the First World War in 1914, in spite of Persia's declared neutrality, the country became the scene of conflict between Russian, Turkish and British forces, which were important factors in the subsequent collapse of the Qajars and the emergence of Riza Khan in 1921. He became the first Pahlavi monarch in 1926.

It must be a tribute to the tenacity of the north west Persian manufactories that they were able to maintain and increase the output in the latter part of the 19th century in spite of the difficult political and economic climate prevailing for much of the time in the province.

NOTES

1 Curzon, op. cit., vol. 1, p. 518.
2 Curzon, op. cit., vol. 1, p. 521.
3 Curzon, op. cit., vol. 1, pp. 528-529.
4 Curzon, op. cit., vol. 1, p. 530.
5 Curzon, op. cit., vol. 1, pp. 524-525.
6 Curzon, op. cit., vol. 1, p. 525.
7 Fraser, *A Winter's Journey*, p. 401, quoted in Curzon, op. cit., vol. 1, p. 523.
8 *The Cambridge History of Islam*, London, 1970, vol. 1, p. 454.
9 Curzon, op. cit., vol. 1, pp. 523-524.
10 Curzon, op. cit., vol. 1, p. 528.
11 Black, D, ed., *World Rugs and Carpets*, London, 1985, p. 134.
12 Lambton, A K S, *Qajar Persia*, London, 1987, p. 223 et seq.

A view over the rooftops of the lower colleges, Süleymaniye complex, Istanbul.

CHAPTER FIVE
THE OTTOMANS

ISTANBUL, the capital of the Ottoman Empire, and adjacent areas form the other major manufacturing source discussed in this work. From a period of expansion and dominance of the Eastern Mediterranean in the 15th to 17th centuries, the Ottoman Empire began to go into slow decline after the treaty of Carlowitz in 1699. This decline was due in part to internal pressures as well as an erosion of military capability, which had become evident in 1683 when the Ottomans failed to capture Vienna.

However, this is not to say that the Empire did not remain a formidable force. It still won military victories, united the whole of the Eastern Mediterranean in an Islamic state and exerted enormous cultural influence. Its decline only became gradually apparent.

Europe in comparison remained fragmented, the various nations frequently changing their allegiances as the situation required. The Ottomans had long been part of this framework of allegiances and up until the end of the 18th century had maintained a close relationship with France, but the advent of Napoleon and his invasion of the Ottoman provinces of Egypt and Palestine obliged them to seek aid elsewhere. Britain and Russia were the obvious counterweight to French aggression.

The Greek revolt in 1821, which carried with it many of those Greeks who held important positions in trade, shipping and administration within the Ottoman Empire, was encouraged by the British, French and Russians alike. By 1830 the Greeks had won independence, which was a major blow to Ottoman trading capability and to the Empire's military and political prestige.

In spite of the Ottomans' alliance with the Russians as a necessary counterweight to Napoleon, the growing power of Russia in fact remained the chief cause of external pressure on the Empire, contesting its influence in the Black Sea and disputing access to the Bosphorus. In this way Russia exemplified the typically ambivalent relationship which the Ottoman Empire had with the Western powers as a whole. Trade in textiles, amongst other goods, illustrates this point. Regardless of political difficulties, Russia was a primary destination for the export of rugs and carpets, on a route which usually led across Persia, and then through the Caucasus and Black Sea area, or even by ship across the Caspian to Baku.

When later in 1833 the Viceroy of Egypt, Muhammad 'Ali, threatened the centre of Ottoman power, Russia went so far as to land troops on the shores of the Bosphorus. This was a measure of direct interference which greatly alarmed the other Western powers. As a first step in countering Russian influence the Convention of London was signed in 1841 which reasserted the Bosphorus as closed to all foreign warships, and in 1856, after Russia's defeat in the Crimean War, further restrictions were placed on Russian advances by the Treaty of Paris. Russia was not again to resume her dominance in affairs with the Ottomans until after the defeat of the French in the Franco-Prussian war of 1871.

The Treaty also provided a measure of Western interference in Ottoman domestic policy by attempting to dictate the Empire's policy towards its Christian citizens. Equal rights with Muslims were demanded, although the Christians were in many cases reluctant to accept the new obligations which this equal citizenship placed upon them.

The increasing military and economic prowess of the West was both envied and feared. During the 19th century, when Ottoman decline became much more evident, there existed within Ottoman society a constant vacillation between attempts to copy Western institutional patterns and a fierce rejection of such patterns. Artistically the Ottomans had shown interest for a long time in Western ideas. Many motifs, of particularly French inspiration,[1] as can be seen in rug design, came to be part of the Turkish artistic tradition.

A series of reforms were initiated by Sultan Selim III at the beginning of the 19th century designed to bring the Empire into the modern age and thus put it on an equal footing with the West. Already the staffing of the Sultan's secular administration, which had previously been supplied solely by Christian recruits, including the very important office of the Grand Vizier, had been increasingly supplanted by a more efficient Muslim bureaucracy. Likewise many of those Muslims responsible for religious affairs, the ulema, had not proved above corruption and had been replaced.

Above all, it had been obvious from the evident decline of the Empire's military capability that the army was in need of modernisation. Although such moves were fiercely resisted by the privileged Janissary corps, often aided in their revolts by the oppressed lower classes, improved officer training and reform of the war industries had been instigated. However, the reforms advocated by Selim led to his deposition by the Janissaries in 1807. His successor, Mustafa IV, who attempted to continue the reforms, was confronted by similar opposition and a further Janissary uprising in the following year resulted in his death.

Only by assuming more autocratic power did Mahmud II (1808-1839) succeed in accomplishing the reforms deemed necessary. The reforms were dubbed the 'Tanzimat' and were encouraged by France and Britain. Mahmud first set about destroying the power of the provincial governors and feudal leaders, then turned his attention to the Janissaries and the ulema. In 1826 the Janissaries were crushed and the leading members of the ulema were subjugated to the Sultan's will. During the reigns of the following sultans, Abdülmecid and Abdülaziz, the reforms continued apace under the direction of leading statesmen like Mustafa Reshid Pasha.

However, the exceedingly important realm of the economy received less attention. Cultivation remained primitive, communications were poor and there was little free capital for investment and the exploitation of natural resources. Peasants were often oppressed by the tax-farmers of state land who set themselves up as landlords. Many traditional crafts and guilds were destroyed by cheap Western imports[2] and Western institutions secured major concessions.

Just as the Ottomans held an ambivalent attitude to the West, so the West was often undecided about the Ottomans. Russian policy, for instance, wavered between weakening and decentralising the Ottoman Empire by political intrigue and directly partitioning Ottoman territory.

The Russians were most consistently opposed by Britain and France. Both wanted to preserve their dominance of the Mediterranean. This was especially important for Britain since it affected the direct route to the East and India. Moreover, the British had a vital trading interest with the Ottoman Empire, in which the balance of trade in Britain's favour was considerable. For example, between 1825-1852 British exports to Turkey increased eight fold and by 1850 Britain exported four times more to Turkey than Turkey exported to Britain. For its part, France had extensive Levantine interests and received a considerable return on loans.

French influence – the wounds of the conflict with Napoleon having healed – was especially prevalent after 1860. Within the governmental structure ministries and a cabinet were established and the provinces were organised according to the French model. Education was likewise reformed on French lines and many youths were sent to the West to be educated.

Pressure from Russia, however, continued to be exerted. As part of the Russian policy of destabilisation Balkan nationalism was actively encouraged in Moldavia, Wallachia and Serbia, which culminated in the formation of the principality of Roumania in 1861. Thereafter, a series of revolts and conflicts in the Balkans led to a Russian invasion of the Ottomans' European possessions and the dismemberment of the European empire in 1878. Nevertheless, Britain made concerted and on the whole successful efforts to restrict Russia's control of the Balkan states.

Similarly, internal pressures had not been resolved by the reforms of the Tanzimat. The advance of a middle-class bureaucracy meant also the rise of a middle-class intelligentsia which resulted in the formation of the Young Ottoman Society in 1865. Their political stance vacillated, but was generally orientated towards a modernised Ottoman nationalism yet still retaining the tenets of Islam. They supported the formation of the Constitution in 1876 but their aims were thwarted when Abdülhamit II took the throne in the same year and suspended the Constitution soon after. This came in the wake of a severe financial crisis – the state was declared bankrupt in 1875 – which resulted directly from the failure of past reforms to tackle the problems of the economic base. An antiquated tax system and the massive interest due on foreign capital loans had finally left the coffers bare. The West henceforth changed its policy of exerting political influence and began a direct annexation of Ottoman territory. At the beginning of the 1880s the British occupied Cyprus and Egypt and the French Tunisia.

Germany did not take part in the physical acquisition of Ottoman territory as a result of the Congress of Berlin, but instead secured financial, technical and trade concessions in Turkey. The Deutsche Bank, for example, later obtained a concession to build the Berlin–Baghdad railway, an agreement which was sealed by the visit of Wilhelm II to Turkey, including a visit to the famous carpet factory at Hereke,[3] and the German military leader, Baron von der Goltz, led the Ottoman army to victory against the Greeks in the Balkans in 1897. This 'military adviser' role followed the precedent set earlier in the century by von Moltke who had played a prominent part in reforming the military structure.

With the accession of Abdülhamit in 1876, there began a long period of autocratic rule from Yıldız Palace, ruthlessly accomplished by an organisation of secret police. Activists of any sort who opposed the Sultan were systematically persecuted, including the Armenians, some of whom had risen to key positions in the administration and financial institutions, part of the influential community that played such an important role in the commissioning and creation of rugs.[4]

As a result of this persecution, those who opposed the Sultan were driven to more radical measures and the revolutionary movement of the Young Turks was formed in 1889, most of its members originating from lower middle-class backgrounds. In 1896 the coup d'état which the Young Turks had been planning was prematurely discovered and they were forced to shift their headquarters to Salonika, where Mustafa Kemal (later to be known as Atatürk) came under their influence.[5] Despite their lack of success they continued to foment revolution and to spread dissent within the army and this culminated in 1908 in a direct revolt which obliged Abdülhamit to restore the Constitution. An attempt to reverse this success was made by the Sultan's supporters in 1909 but it ended in failure. The Sultan was finally deposed in favour of Mehmed V.

The Young Turks' particular brand of nationalism was not entirely progressive. They ruled by means of a one-party system. In many respects they instigated positively reactionary policies, especially with regard to the minority population of Armenians, who were subject to persecutions and massacre. On the other hand educational policies for girls, who were given for the first time much wider opportunities, exemplified their more progressive reforms.

After the Young Turk revolution in 1908, in spite of German support and British opposition to Russian annexation, the Empire gradually lost more of its Balkan territory. Bulgaria declared independence, and by 1913, after a series of wars against the Balkan league of states, almost the whole of the Empire's European possessions had been lost. The same fate befell its North African territory, which was conceded in the war with Italy from 1911 to 1912.

During the First World War the Ottomans' associations with Germany and fear of the Russians led to their participation on the German side. Despite dogged resistance by the Ottomans in many of their territories, of which Gallipoli was the most outstanding example and where Mustafa Kemal came to prominence as a commander, they suffered inevitable defeat with the surrender of Germany. There followed occupation by Britain, France and Italy, and, most humiliating of all, the invasion of Izmir by the Greeks. The Sultan still remained nominally in power and, under Allied protection, used this period to extend the persecution of his enemies. It is remarkable that under the conditions which prevailed prior to and just after the end of the First World War the Armenian community, who were frequent victims of persecution, still managed to produce the wonderful creations exemplified by the ateliers of Kumkapı.

Mustafa Kemal now became a focus for much of the nationalistic feeling which had been aroused by the occupation and hardened by the Sultan's ruthless measures. Although the Sultan rigorously tried to crush all opposition, forces under Kemal began to gain ground. A series of successes enabled them to rid the country of foreign occupation, the Greeks finally being expelled in 1922. For a time rival governments existed in Ankara and Istanbul. The country was, however, much more strongly behind the nationalists who, after declaring a republic, sent the Sultan into exile in 1924. The new government then instigated a series of reforms, which influenced Riza Khan in Persia, that radically altered the institutional structures of Turkish society. Thus was instigated the final phase of the modernisation of Turkey on Western lines, something which had originally been envisaged by the Tanzimat, albeit in a substantially different form.

NOTES

1 There are a number of fine Hereke silk rugs in private collections based entirely on French designs. See also Beattie, op. cit., p. 130, and G Goodwin, *Ottoman Turkey*, London, 1977, p. 21.

2 See above, p. 15, and p. 16, note 4.

3 Beattie, op. cit., pp. 130-131.

4 See Beattie, op. cit., pp. 129-130, for the Armenian role in the establishment of the factory at Hereke: and for the Armenian role in general, der Manuelian, L, and Eiland, M L, *Weavers, Merchants and Kings*, Fort Worth, 1984.

5 Armstrong, H C, *Grey Wolf: Mustafa Kemal – An intimate study of a dictator*, London, 1932, p. 25 et seq.

The Sultan Ahmet Mosque, known as the Blue Mosque, Istanbul, one of the greatest monuments of the Ottoman capital. It was designed by Mehmet Ağa and constructed between 1609 and 1617.

The kiosk on the waterfront at Hereke, built in honour of the visit by Kaiser Wilhelm II in 1898 to the imperial manufactories. It was furnished with the finest work of the ateliers. Today it is still an important showpiece for visitors to the Sümerbank manufactory.

1 PERSIA
North West Persian Silk Prayer Rug

Dated 1313 AH/1895 AD

This exceptionally fine work is a masterpiece of the school of north west Persia which incorporates all the great elements of the age. The north west had political influence which derived from its position as one of strategic importance close to the borders of Ottoman Turkey and Tsarist Russia. Within the province there remained the powerful influence and entrepreneurial spirit of the Armenian community which was responsible for much of the trading in these superb hand-created works.

This beautiful rug is dominated by the peacock blue main field which is adorned by a series of columns that support an arch. Of significance is the fact that the piece bears an inscription, 1313, equivalent to 1895, which is picked out in fine white lettering in the lower right-hand part of the field and is shown laterally inverted, to preserve symmetry, on the left-hand side also.

The border contains a series of yellow and madder medallions on an indigo field. Within the medallions are a series of small signs which might be interpreted as numerals. Interspersed about the medallions are a series of small flower motifs which resemble vines. Such decorative features are common throughout the Islamic period in Persia, especially in the magnificent stucco work which occurs as early as the 10th century in a number of important mosques. There is also evidence that such motifs were also a familiar part of the Sasanian artistic repertoire. The medallions also echo features found on Persian manuscripts and other notable museum examples of rugs attributed to central Persia during the Safavid period. The guardbands, of which the inner series are narrower, show a somewhat stylised tendency and feature groups of blossoming plants.

The main design is of four intricate and beautiful columns with half columns to the sides. Between the columns are a series of very fine lamps with pendants with a larger lamp shown centrally. These are finely drawn in golds and madder with various floral and vegetal finials. The arch has a scalloped edge and above the ivory spandrels are a series of scrolls and palmettes in madder and blue. These are all features which have an architectonic precedence. The floral devices from the base of the main field also hint at the tree of life design which was to become a popular, familiar feature. The vase portrayed suggests the same tendency. These motifs were popular also on tile work which adorned palaces as well as religious buildings.

Although this magnificent rug might loosely be described as a prayer rug, it was probably never used as such and should be regarded rather as a column rug and possibly be linked to similarly derived examples, of which the more important examples extant today are those usually associated with the Turkish Empire. The function of such rugs was almost certainly to be part of the internal wall furnishings of a mansion, and as such are associated with architectonic arcades and facades. Upon the usually bare walls such prominent design and harmony of colour would have been an enduring and movable work of art which progressed with the passage of the seasons from one part of the building to another.

REFERENCES

No adequate study exists for prayer rugs of the period. However, for a discussion of the development of the genre see Erdmann, K, *Oriental Carpets*, London, 1960, and *Seven Hundred Years of Oriental Carpets*, Berkeley, 1970; also Bode, W von, and Kühnel, E, *Antique Rugs from the Near East*, trans. C G Ellis, London, 1970.

STRUCTURE
size: 188 x 138 cm
weft: Cotton, 3 strands
weft colour: Natural
warp: Silk, 4 strands
warp colour: Natural
side cords: Silk, 1 strand
side cords colour: New indigo
ends: Nil
knots: Symmetrical, short floss silk
dyes: Vegetable
knot count: 23 x 23 = 529 per sq in
total: 2,113,884

2 PERSIA
North West Persian Silk Prayer Rug

Late 19th Century

This is another superb rug which, in design, is related to the previous example. Originally from the same productive area of north west Persia, it is a further example of the artistic inventiveness of the masters in silk of the province of Azarbaijan.

The main field is composed of a tranquil rose madder which bears a series of columns and the arch usually associated with the prayer niche.

The border has a series of stylised medallions utilising a palette of ivory, turquoise and rose madder on an indigo field. The main border is protected by double guardbands to either side which have a design of small flowers and tendrils on a madder ground.

The main field has ivory spandrels which feature a series of vegetal and floral motifs in indigo, ivory and madder. The four columns supporting the main field are adorned with a series of diamonds which hint at the Qajar use of inlaid wood. The bases of the columns are in ivory with floral appendages and introduce a pistachio green into the palette, whilst the capitals also feature the use of indigo flowerheads which continue to form part of the design of the spandrels. There are four side lamps with a larger central lamp. The last named descends almost to the very bottom of the main field, where it becomes like a vase growing from the base of the field. The shape of the main blossom from this main vase-like feature hints at the three-pointed crown of the Qajar kings.

As with the previous example, the use of this rug was probably as part of the interior furnishings of a major house. As such, it is also related to building facades. It contains those elements of stylised arabesques which were popular during the great period of the Safavids. As such, the rug shows a continuing and imaginative use of those designs allied to the astounding skills of the silk masters of the north west.

REFERENCES

See references to plate 1. For the crown motif see various paintings found in Falk, S J, *Qajar Paintings*, London, 1972.

STRUCTURE

size: 190 x 138 cm
weft: Cotton, 1 strand
weft colour: Natural
warp: Cotton, 1 strand
warp colour: Natural
side cords: Silk, 1 strand
side cords colour: New red
ends: Nil
knots: Symmetrical, short floss silk
dyes: Vegetable
knot count: 16 x 16 = 256 per sq in
total: 1,036,800

3 PERSIA
North West Persian Silk Prayer Rug
Late 19th Century

This unusually striking and beautiful rug is another manufacture of the seemingly unfathomable reservoir of skills of late 19th century north west Persia.

The main field is a light pistachio green with columns. There are also stylised scrolling arabesques in old gold with floral details in madder, indigo and ivory with an arch at the top of the field.

The main border contains a series of elaborate and stylised palmettes joined by finely crafted thin tendrils and smaller leaves and blossoms. The guardbands to either side have an indigo field with more stylised vegetal features in ivory and madder.

As with the previous examples, the immediate form of the rug suggests that of a prayer rug, although its use as such must be questioned. The most exciting and innovative feature is the free standing and central column which has engaged columns to either side of the field which support the arch section directly. These columns have the most unusual feature of a bricked design picked out in blue and madder with white pointing. The bases and capitals of the columns are in madder and indigo.

It is the central feature of the single column which strikes one for it is rather as if this column, which unites along its axis the arabesque of the field, is derived from a vase motif of which this is the evolved elongated element. It may also suggest garden features, as though the niche itself is a panel or a window giving us a view of a paradise. The use of free standing columns is not a familiar one within Persia, although there are such examples from a foreign contribution in Afghanistan and other areas to the east.

As well as its unusual design, this is also a rug harmoniously designed and executed to a high degree of technical excellence.

REFERENCES

A viewpoint on the tree of life motif can be found in Ackermann, P, 'Three Early 16th Century Tapestries', *The Rockefeller McCormick Collection*, (series of catalogues), Chicago, 1932.

STRUCTURE

size: 151 x 234 cm
weft: Silk, 6 strands
weft colour: Natural
warp: Silk, floss
warp colour: Natural
side cords: Cotton, 2 strands
side cords colour: Oversewn with red silk
ends: Nil
knots: Symmetrical, long floss silk
dyes: Vegetable
knot count: 18 x 18 = 324 per sq in
total: 1,758,672

4 PERSIA
North West Persian Silk Prayer Rug

Late 19th Century

Probably associated with the provincial capital of Tabriz, this is a striking and handsome example of a silk prayer rug from the middle Qajar period. It is likely that such superb examples became increasingly sought after towards the end of the last century when the local workshops were called upon to produce their finest work for a growing market.

The main field is of a superb copper red which makes the rug truly powerful and impressive. The field supports the stepped spandrels of the mihrab arch with two narrow and elegant columns with a lamp descending into the centre. The main border contains a series of stylised rosettes with pairs of long wide leaves in a design familiar over a long period and associated very much with this area.

To either side of the border are a pair of guardbands with rosette and leaf design on a diminishing scale.

The central design also features around the bottom and sides of the main field a series of delicate and fine blossoms which project unobtrusively into the main field; the elegant and narrow columns and rosette and leaf design recalling the border. The spandrels have an indigo field to contrast with the main field and carry a whole series of blossoms arranged in bunches which, at first glance, also resemble the pomegranate. The stepped edge of the spandrels, as well as the rows of blossoms within, suggest the stalactiting which is such an important and consistent feature of the arch in Islamic architecture. Hanging from the apex of the mihrab is the lamp containing nine blossoms and suspended from a very finely wrought chain. The lamp is the familiar feature found before the mihrab in the mosque and which recalls those verses in the Qur'an where the mihrab, the niche indicating the direction of prayer, is referred to as a niche for lights.

In contrast to the previous rugs which have the form of the prayer niche, the elegant simplicity of this superb work suggests its main use was to be as a prayer rug. Compared with those examples it remains more faithful to the architectonic precedents of the mihrab, although whether such a work of exquisite quality was ever used as a *sajjada* is questionable. More likely such work, as with most fine silk rugs, was regarded as a valued family treasure and would have been rarely used. This example also contrasts, in terms of its artistry and technical excellence, with a more familiar group of prayer rugs associated with Tabriz and which are characterised by light pastel shades. It would seem here that the masterweaver responsible has been concerned to project into his work a degree of honesty, discipline and individuality which marks it off as exceptional.

REFERENCES

For the likely Turkish precedents of this style of rug see Erdmann, op. cit., and Bode and Kühnel, op. cit.

STRUCTURE

size: 129 x 166 cm
weft: Silk, 2 strands
weft colour: Pale madder
warp: Silk, 2 strands
warp colour: Natural
side cords: Silk, 1 strand
side cords colour: Pale madder
ends: Nil
knots: Symmetrical, short floss silk
dyes: Vegetable
knot count: 18 x 18 = 324 per sq in
total: 1,074,060

5 PERSIA
Tabriz Silk Prayer Rug

Late 19th Century

This is a superb example of the pastel type which was apparently so instrumental in shaping the taste of a great generation of collector dealers at the end of the last century. The style and especially the distinctive colouring was a response by the masters of the north west to the demand for luxury wealth items from the East.

The ivory main field is one of endless subtlety which moves with the change in light chameleon-like through shades of silver and white. It is surmounted by the restrained colouring of the arches of the prayer arch which is notably pointed and is supported on thin columns. Suspended centrally is the familiar lamp which is a necessity in this style of work; not only are lamps a feature of actual mihrabs but they recall for the faithful the esoteric Qur'anic verses referring to the mihrab as a niche for lights – *mishkat al-anwar*. These elements are rendered in a delicate but precise manner anticipating the style of art deco. There is a frieze at the top recalling architectonic precedents. The frieze has a decoration recalling in a stylised form the designs frequently found in mihrabs and rendered in superb, complex carved stucco, notably from the period of the Great Saljuqs onwards (i.e. post 1032). The delicate lattice in the spandrels also seems an attempt to render the complex stucco stalactiting seen particularly on mihrabs.

The overall design owes much to the important group of prayer rugs usually associated with Turkish centres such as Ladik and Gördes from the 17th and 18th centuries. The borders are wide and complex with traditional leaf and flower motifs in thin and elegant madder lines on an ivory field. There are five guardbands to either side. The four inner are of a madder vegetal design on ivory whilst the outer ones have a tiny arabesque leaf in indigo.

This is a primary example of an important and significant group of rugs from the Tabriz area during this period. As they were much in demand they were sought after by the great collectors and dealers of the time.

REFERENCES
For the Qur'anic reference, see XXIV: 35.

STRUCTURE
size: 169 x 118 cm
weft: Silk, 2 strands
weft colour: Natural
warp: Silk, 2 strands
warp colour: Natural
side cords: Silk, 4 strands
side cords colour: Natural
ends: Nil
knots: Symmetrical, short floss silk
dyes: Vegetable
knot count: 16 x 16 = 256 per sq in
total: 791,488

CHAPTER SIX
THE CULTURAL MILIEU

ONE of the great problems in discussing the background to the creation of oriental rugs is obtaining a clear idea of the social conditions which pertained at the time. There is most often information available for general classes and transactions within society, such as court and administrative records, and frequently personal descriptions of upper class figures. Yet little exists on the conditions of the weavers, their thoughts and feelings, their cultural aspirations. In the absence of records at the time we can do little more than tease out facts from oblique references in official documents or rely on passing accounts from Western observers.

Of course, there is always recourse to examining life as it presently exists in order to deduce that which may constitute an ongoing tradition, but with the pace of Western influence constantly increasing and the old ways being discarded this is no more reliable than looking for a true image in a distorted mirror.

We can observe certain cultural habits in existence today which can be corroborated against accounts from the past.[1] There exist in Eastern society strong rituals of social behaviour, as clearly delineated as the day is marked off by calls to prayer which nowadays sound from the loudspeakers of the mosque and the street. One of the strongest contrasts we encounter coming from our Western society with its emphasis on sexuality and sexual roles is the status of women. In the Middle East, men and women are very much segregated into 'public' and 'private' domains. For the most part it is men who perform the public duties, except in the more Westernised regions. Men are waiters in restaurants and cafés, drivers, bazaar sellers, bus conductors, office clerks, typists of official letters, police. Women provide the fundamentals for this public duty to be performed. Often in the countryside they are to be seen working the land or in city cafés one can hear their voices from the kitchen and the busy sounds of food preparation. In town houses they move behind windows or usher children in from the street.

The same contrast is to be found in the process of manufacturing. It is the women and young girls who most regularly provide the physical labour of tying knots day after day. Men, however, sometimes but rarely in the company of the woman who has completed the work, sell the finished article, hawking it around from shop to shop, bargaining with the dealers. In a city situation the men purchase the silk or wool which provides the material for the women. Most often the women knot in a back room of their houses or perhaps on a balcony of a city flat; a few may be employed by local dealers or by larger factories, as at Hereke in Turkey, where the position of supervisor is occupied by a man.

Such 'front' and 'back' aspects of society extend also to the social situation. When guests arrive, men remain sitting with male guests on carpets in the main living quarters while the women retreat to a back room or kitchen. Quite often the men will be served food or drink entirely separately from the women, sitting on the floor on carpets with a circular cloth drawn over feet and knees and central communal dishes for food. If women do join in the same meal they are always the servers, always ready to pour tea from the brewing pot.

The wishes of the guest are paramount. It is a disgrace for him to have to pay for anything in the host's company. He is accompanied everywhere, whatever he desires, within respectable bounds of course, is obtained for him and his wishes govern all choices. Socialising thus places heavy obligations on guests and hosts alike which we in the West may find restrictive and unusually ritualised.

Another aspect of Middle Eastern society, and probably most societies outside the affluent West, is the extent to which children are involved in work. The young girls are frequently involved in knotting as well as all the chores of the household, often from a very early age. A Hereke dealer testified to the fact that one of the accomplished knotters in the area was a girl of five years old![2] Within the public domain the boys are readily to be seen as conductors on the buses, shoe shiners, guides, carpet sellers and hawkers of all sorts. This is a necessity, of course, in a strongly hierarchical society of much material poverty. Ordinary village life is in the main extremely simple: a family owns a small plot of land and perhaps a few animals. Their dwelling is plain and the few rooms are furnished with carpets, nowadays mostly machine-made since hand-knotted items are expensive, and low sofas which double as beds but little other furniture.

In general the majority of sustained labour is performed by the women. Men have much more recognisable leisure. Men frequently gather in cafés to drink tea, play backgammon and enjoy each other's company. Women restrict their socialising to visiting each other's houses. On certain family occasions visits are made to parks, gardens and open spaces, especially if situated near the cool flow of running water. Carpets and rugs are spread and cooking implements, dishes and food are unpacked.

To a visitor's eye much of the economy is connected with the bazaar. In the big towns there are intricate mazes of thousands of shops along narrow streets. The whole population seems to be involved in selling. Hawkers and criers are everywhere. Some shops specialise but many contain such a variety of wares that it is difficult to find space to move or to understand how the shopkeeper is able to keep track of his merchandise. It is the kind of society where you know that anything you ever wanted for the construction or mending of an article can be found. One of the most obvious factors of employment within the bazaar is the apparent overmanning. Each shop appears to have an excess of employees, standing, sitting, talking. Many of them employ 'hustlers' whose job it is to persuade people in off the street, so that outside there is a constant bustle and noise of interaction. Even so, one suspects that the majority of custom available to such obvious duplication of outlets is obtained through friends and relatives.

Then there is the elasticity of time which is apparent inside any of the shops of the bazaar. Hours are spent sitting around drinking tea, gazing at the street or indulging occasionally in quiet conversation, and sales are unhurried, leisurely activities despite sudden bursts of bargaining. However, this in no way detracts from the relative efficiency of operations. It is not uncommon at bus stations for buses to go on time; things get done; people keep appointments.

Another cultural tradition which has not yet been totally superseded by Western influence is the love of strong colour and ornament. Many theories may be advanced as to why this is so: perhaps in order to relieve the senses of much of the tedium resident in an often harsh and monotonous landscape, perhaps the rich availability of natural colours and dyes, spices and roots, perhaps as a Qur'an inspired celebration of God's

bounty. Or is it simply as van Gogh found, transferring from his dour environment of the Borinage and Brabant where his forbidding masterpiece *The Potato Eaters*[3] was painted to the glorious sundrenched area of Provence, that in bright sunlight colours burst into life and almost physically vibrate to the eye, so that only a blind man could ignore them? It should not be forgotten that strong colouring in art has been a feature of the area since Classical times. Those clean, plain facades and statuary which we associate predominantly with Greek civilisation and the romance of ruins were, in fact, once highly decorated, like Egyptian artefacts had been. Whatever the reason for their origins, cultural attributes like these have survived down the centuries in spite of the West's attempts to erode them and only now are they in danger of collapsing completely. Even so, the rise of a new fundamentalism may yet have some effect in art.

But what we can deduce from a present culture does not fully explain what went before. What kind of a society did the ordinary knotters of carpets and rugs experience in the last century? We have touched on some of these ideas in the sections on the Qajars and the

A Western view of an Eastern bazaar.

Ottomans but not really said how things existed for ordinary people.

Society was much more rigid in organisation than it is today. Each rank was clearly designated, even down to the kind of clothes that it was permitted to wear. This was so also in death where in Turkey a turban on a gravestone indicated a man's station in life. Transfer between classes was rare, rendering the society peculiarly static, but it was generally understood that favour and high office, for those within reach of it, could be bought. Naturally this made bribery and corruption commonplace.[4] Cruel punishments, particularly amongst the ruling classes where hideous fates awaited those who presented a challenge to power, were frequently meted out. Witness the blinding or wholesale slaughter of possible heirs to the throne by newly ascendant Ottoman sultans and Persian shahs.

The economy was based upon peasant production and was only slowly superseded towards the end of the 19th century by Western industrial practices. Resources, as has been pointed out, were largely left unexploited. The Sultan and the Shah were the supreme authorities within their respective countries and carried that epithet like the Qajar rulers of 'the shadow of God upon earth', although their actions were monitored by religious officials, such as the Chief Mufti (*shaykh al-Islam*) within the Ottoman Empire.

For the mass of the common people, however, including the manufacturers of rugs, recognising the supreme authority of the Sultan or Shah and also that of senior clerical figures did not also rule out the adherence to a host of popular superstitions which clung to the periphery of the Islamic faith. Such superstitions included the existence of angels and jinns, who were fiery spirits which behaved much like humans. Some jinns were deemed benevolent, but others, led by Iblis, the fallen angel, were evil in intent and needed to be driven off by lucky charms. Charms which were considered especially powerful consisted of written extracts from the Qur'an often worn round the neck or burnt in the wick of a candle, and coloured glass balls as a protection against the Evil Eye.[5] Ornamented balls were frequently hung in gateways of buildings. In carpet manufacturing it is popularly said that knotters included in each carpet one imperfection at least to avoid the envy of the Evil Eye. Another favourite charm was the ostrich eggs brought back by those returning from the Hajj. With such strong beliefs extant among the people it is not surprising to find comparable features in many rugs. Sacrifices were also commonplace in offering thanks for things like recovering from illness, undergoing successful circumcision, or completing the building of a mosque.

There were also in existence orders of dervishes, formed mostly by mystics in the 12th to 13th centuries with the avowed aim of approaching God more closely. They propagated Muhammad's 'secret' teachings, not those from the Hadith (the Traditions of the Prophet), and these teachings provided the formulae for the organisation of the various sects and secret societies. In addition, the patron 'saints' of many guilds were revered members of the dervishes and artisans often belonged to lodges of a particular sect. Some guilds, however, adopted Hebrew patriarchs, the supposed originators of their trade, or companions of the Prophet. Seth was the patron saint of weavers in Turkey.[6]

Because the dervishes were much more accessible to the common people and perhaps because some of their rituals were outside the stricter practices of the mainstream Islamic faith, the dervishes were very popular amongst poorer people. However, each order possessed a different kind of religious formulation so that the Bektashi indulged in rather loose rites whereas the Mevlevi, with their centre on Konya and their reverence of Jalal al-Din Rumi the famous poet and mystical teacher, were much more strict and intellectual in their approach. Whatever their sect, dervishes were generally treated with respect, although E G Browne in his *A Year Amongst the Persians* tells a few stories which would have us believe otherwise.[7] The Sultan of Ottoman Turkey at least treated them with respect, knowing that their hold over the common people placed them in a useful position for control and mediation.

Coupled with the belief in spirits was the apportioning of special significance to certain holy places such as wells, rivers, mountains and tombs of saints. Generally these were supervised by a dervish who received contributions provided by thankful pilgrims for cures of illness, infertility and similar problems.

In the towns working life was fairly strictly controlled by the guilds, which were highly developed in Turkey. The system began to break down towards the end of the 19th century under the weight of foreign imports. Each guild had a responsibility for its own particular trade, issuing licences and papers and setting standards for transactions. Until the system began to break down imports were also generally under the guild officials' control so that restrictions could be placed on any imports which undercut locally produced goods. However, because guilds exercised such important duties in the protection of their members it also meant that there existed little mobility between trades.

Crafts were exercised under concessions and monopolies, with a specified number of craftsmen allowed to operate. Men registered their tools and goods and there were fixed areas of trade and a fixed number

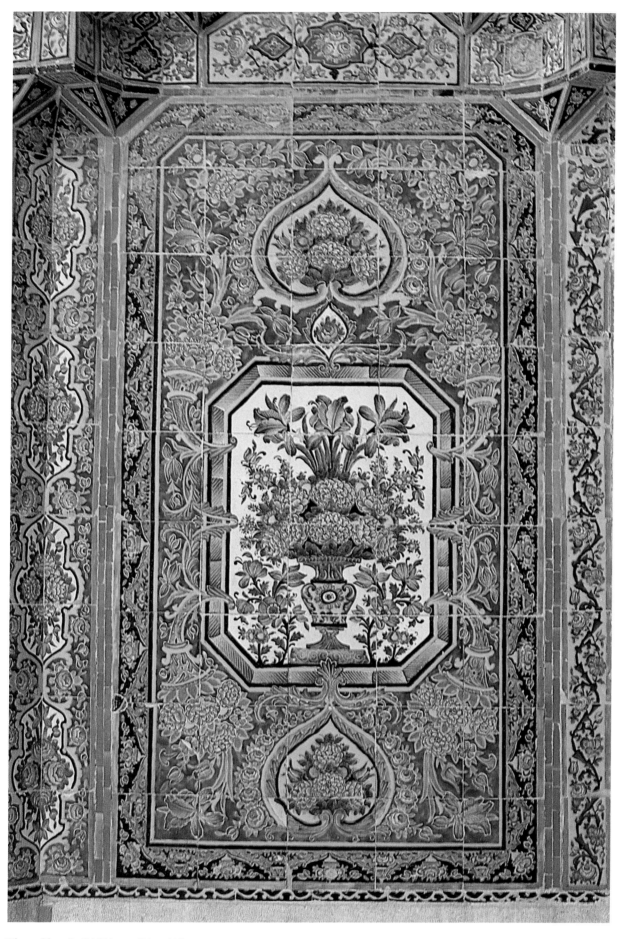

Tile panel from the Vakil Mosque, Shiraz, 18th century, showing the Eastern predilection for rich colour.

of shops. Any transfer to a son or relative had to be verified by the guild. Throughout the guilds strict codes of work were enforced in the name of security which resisted innovation and new techniques, resulting in the frequent reworking of old themes. Since art was controlled by the guilds, there therefore existed a constancy of taste and technique and high workmanship which was not subject to the flux of individual genius as in the West. This is readily apparent in the creation of rugs and is as much a religious concept as a feature of trade protection. In such situations it is only the genius for subtle variation and a mastery of technique which can avoid stagnation and it is apparent that at various periods of rug creation the stagnation has not easily been avoided.

Guilds consisted of masters, journeymen and apprentices and recognised a rigid hierarchy under a shaykh. They appear to have been exclusive of women. Any women weavers must presumably have been operating then only as adjuncts of organised designers and craftsmen within guilds. The guilds organised their own discipline, expulsion being an effective deterrent in such a closed situation. Monthly or weekly contributions were made by members and loans were often extended, including those for welfare benefits and funeral expenses, very much like the arrangements trade unions made in the West during the latter part of the 19th century. In addition, donations were given to worthy causes, for example, orphans, and religious activities within the guild's local area. The apprentices were attached to a master from whom they learnt their trade. The former apprentice graduated in turn when he finally exhibited his 'masterpiece'. On this occasion the established masters paid large sums over and above the real cost of the article in order to give the former apprentice enough capital to start his own business.

Every ten or twenty years within the Ottoman Empire there occurred a joint guild festivity consisting of an excursion and picnic in the countryside. Exhibits of the masters' work were displayed in processions on special public occasions and the finest examples were presented to the Sultan. We have beautiful pictorial representations of such events as in the *Sûrname* now in the Topkapı Palace and it would be interesting to speculate that some of the finest rugs may have been presented to the Sultan in such ceremonies.

The Sultan's demand for excellence often brought members of guilds living in the east of the country to Istanbul. In fact, the interchange of artists within the Islamic sphere frequently occurred. Persian weavers influenced the output of Turkey; Turks travelled to Persia, Iraq and Egypt; workers came to Turkey from Damascus, Aleppo and Samarkand, especially under Süleyman when many artists were

assembled at his court.[8] Of all the arts within the Ottoman Empire architecture was the most rich and flourishing, and it is therefore not surprising to see many architectural features informing the decoration of rugs. Most art depicting animal or human figures was reserved for the sultans and upper class connoisseurs in order not to offend public sensibility.

As in the present day, 19th century society was organised around the patriarchal domination of the extended family. Women hardly ventured out. Servants did any necessary public duties, including shopping, for the wealthy, although there were occasions when parties of women under the watchful eye of a eunuch were seen visiting the bazaar.[9] In poorer families such public duties were generally performed by husbands or male children. Women's lives were probably more confined than they are today. A visit to the hammam (the local bath) or in a group, bearing gifts and sweetmeats, to friends or neighbours being the sole relaxation from confinement, as indeed was the family outing, in a caique (boat) or covered ox cart, if the family were rich enough. Caiques were the preferred method of transport in Istanbul, intersected as it is by water. Passengers sat on carpets and cushions, the men and women separate. Fares were fixed and no overloading was allowed, a practice which accords very much with the present day regulations set on the dolmuş in Istanbul. This outing to a park or garden with cooling water is witnessed by Lady Mary Wortley Montagu and is still much in evidence today and it is therefore not surprising that the garden is one of the most frequent elements in rug design (see particularly plates 21 and 22).

However, in the arrangement of marriages the boy's mother was placed in a position of considerable power. She had the right to inspect any prospective matches, and this was sometimes done at the hammam.[10] Amongst poorer families such negotiations and inspections would have been minimal. The trousseau prepared for the girl, as well as containing clothes and linen, would frequently have contained family heirlooms and undoubtedly rugs.

Death by disease was a frequent hazard of living in towns. The death rate in places like Istanbul was especially high, much of it occurring because of frequent outbreaks of plague, including cholera and typhoid. Many inhabitants of the city attempted to escape such ravages by sailing to the islands in the Bosphorus. There were many superstitious medical practices attempted in the face of such outbreaks. After death, cypresses were often planted in the graveyards, symbols of immortality carried by their evergreen leaves, and their resinous smell believed an antidote to death (see plate 21 and p. 92). Before death, cures were attempted by appeasing the fiery jinns or the Evil Eye, perhaps by pouring lead, or burning hairs, or sweeping seven shops. Herbal cures were often effected, such as aniseed for the digestion, or rhubarb as a laxative.[11] It would not be surprising then to find representations of such beneficial plant life within rug decoration.

Most artisans' houses, at least in Istanbul, were small and plain. Whereas the richer elements of society may have possessed large houses with courtyards and a central garden, the lower floors barred against passing observers and the upper storeys projecting out over the street, the houses of artisans were often single-storeyed constructions of wood. This resulted in a great risk of fire, especially when one considers the use of the *tandır*, and attempts were made in Istanbul to ban the use of wood as a construction material. However, they availed little and at frequent intervals fires continued to ravage the city,[12] very much as earthquakes frequently ravaged Tabriz. Persian houses reflected in style the different climate. There was little use of wood: mud brick, with baked brick in the better houses, being the usual building medium. Most houses were single storeyed, looking inwards on a courtyard and presenting a blank facade to the outside to ensure privacy and seclusion.

The women's quarters were situated furthest from the street and were comparatively small. They were perhaps divided by a curtain from the general living room. Like many working class areas in the West at the time, sanitation was extremely limited. Slops and rubbish were usually disposed of in the streets.

Ordinary family houses possessed little furniture: perhaps a few rugs, mattresses, a cooking stove, pots and pans. Rugs were the most frequently used and popular. Travellers nearly always carried a rolled carpet.[13] The wealthier families had low sofas and cushions and perhaps a finer carpet hung like a tapestry upon the wall. As at the present day, shoes were removed at the door and carpets were sat on, slept on and prayed on. In summer the carpets were often replaced with rush mats and in poorer quarters the floor was of beaten earth. Heating was provided by the *tandır* – a quilt over hot coals – in Turkey or the *kursi* in Persia. Both richer and poorer houses provided little distinction between bedrooms and living quarters.

NOTES

1 See below, pp. 93-99.

2 Information supplied by John Orley from interviews in Hereke in 1987.

3 See, for example, Gaunt, W, *The Impressionists*, London, 1970, p. 130.

4 For a flavour of this, see Morier, J, *The Adventures of Hajji Baba of Ispahan*, London, 1824 (rep. 1914).

5 Lewis, R, *Everyday Life in the Ottoman Empire*, London, 1971, pp. 52-54. See also Lane, E, *The Manners and Customs of the Modern Egyptians*, London, 1908 (rep. 1966), pp. 257-269, for detailed descriptions of superstitions prevalent in the Islamic world.

6 See Lewis, op. cit., p. 149.

7 Browne, op. cit., London, 1983, new ed.; see, for example, pp. 195-198. There were also numerous professional holy men whose behaviour might best be described as scandalous, rather as certain groups of religious mendicants earned a bad reputation in Medieval Europe. For various anecdotes related to this see especially Safi's, *Lata'if-i Tava'if*.

8 See Lewis, op. cit., p. 151 et seq, and Kühnel, E, *Islamic Arts*, trans. K Watson, London, 1970, pp. 29, 171; also Bensoussan, op. cit., p. 34. Since the time of Mehmet the Conqueror European artists had also frequently been attracted to Istanbul: see especially Çelik, Z, *The Remaking of Istanbul*, Seattle and London, 1986, p. 52, for the presence of architects in the 19th century.

9 Gautier, T, *Constantinople of To-day*, trans. R Howe Gould, London, 1854, p. 123.

10 Lewis, op. cit., p. 100.

11 Lewis, op. cit., p. 107.

12 See Çelik, op. cit., p. 52 et seq.

13 See, for example, Gautier, op. cit., pp. 42, 73-74.

6 PERSIA
Kashan Silk Medallion Rug
Late 19th Century

Kashan had a long history in rug manufacturing from the Safavid period on, although the manufactories seemed depressed from the fall of the Safavids in the early 18th century until the latter part of the 19th. The fame and prestige of central Persia for its silk masterweavings was also turned to producing traditional rugs deriving from great classical motifs. This example demonstrates the use of a medallion and corner piece design adapted to a later age and artistic sensibilities.

The main field bears its design on a field of mellow ivory. On the field are medallions and corner pieces with areas full of blossoms, principally in rose madder and pistachio green.

The main border with its pistachio green echoes elements in the main field: its blossoms and palmettes of varying sizes and sprays of flowers using a palette mainly of brown, gold and rose pink. The overall effect of the border is of a light, spacious, uncluttered and refreshing design.

The guardbands to either side of the border are the same. They have a brown ground with a decoration of tiny rosette, leaf and tendril. The main design is dominated by the multi-lobed medallion with pendants; the latter containing fields of indigo. Upon the pistachio field of the medallion is a lattice in rose pink with a central rosette, other floral devices and finials. The corner pieces extend to run continuously around all sides. Their scalloped edges extend into scroll work, whilst the mauve fields of the corner pieces are filled with other small flowers.

The design of medallion and corner pieces is a long established one in the Persian knotting tradition and is strongly associated with Safavid precedents. Design precedents are also seen in other disciplines such as bookbindings, as well as in internal decorations such as wall panels and ceilings. The lattice and central rosette upon the main medallion also recall features which in due course are associated with the work of Ferahan (see plate 19).

REFERENCES

For the manufactory of Kashan in the modern period see Edwards, C, *The Persian Carpet*, London, 1933. For the great medallion carpets of the Safavid period see, for example, the works shown in *The Eastern Carpet in the Western World*, London, 1983, pp. 84-90.

STRUCTURE
size: 126 x 196 cm
weft: Cotton, 5 strands
weft colour: Green
warp: Silk, 2 strands
warp colour: Natural
side cords: Silk, 1 strand
side cords colour: Mauve
ends: Nil
knots: Asymmetrical, short floss silk
dyes: Vegetable
knot count: 16 x 16 = 256 per sq in
total: 985,600

7 PERSIA
North West Persian Silk Medallion Rug

Late 19th Century

Having the advantage of the magnificent precedents of the Safavid period, the masterweavers of north west Persia were constantly seeking to adapt and modify existing design forms. This medallion rug shows just such an extension of a traditional design.

The main field is a magnificent copper red which supports the main medallion as well as a host of blossoms and leaves, mainly in ivory and various shades of blue and indigo.

The border with its ivory field has a series of madder rosettes with leaves and tendrils picked out in madder and indigo.

Protecting the border and main field are the identical guardbands which have a design of leaf and flowerhead, somewhat stylised, and which suggest the form of a cartouche. This fine piece is dominated by the central elongated medallion in ivory, its lanceolate extensions along the main axis with fields of indigo. Centrally is a multi-lobed rosette with a central floral feature. Within the main medallion is a series of flowers in which the use of indigo is to be noted. The medallion is surrounded by a series of looping, long leaves about which are the scrolling tendrils and mass of small blossoms and leaves which extend throughout the whole field.

Although there are many precedents for the medallion rug, the artist here in creating such an unusual medallion has shown the constant inventiveness of the workshops of this amazingly fruitful part of Persia.

REFERENCES

For classical precedents with medallion and lattice design see Beattie, M, *Carpets of Central Persia*, London, 1976, p. 63 et seq.

STRUCTURE

size: 128 x 202 cm
weft: Silk, 1 strand
weft colour: Red
warp: Silk, 3 strands
warp colour: Natural
side cords: Silk, tape
side cords colour: New red
ends: Nil
knots: Symmetrical, short floss silk
dyes: Vegetable
knot count: 20 x 20 = 400 per sq in
total: 1,616,000

8 PERSIA
North West Persian Silk Rug

Mid 19th Century

The north west province was important not only as a manufacturing area and a major entrepot but it was also a politically vital area for the Qajars. Often the heir apparent was appointed as the province's governor and the Qajars maintained important links with the region. Because of the royal emblem seen on this rug it is likely that the dynasty was also commissioning the finest manufactures of the region during the 19th century.

The main field has a beautiful madder ground on which are depicted four multi-lobed medallions. These are in ivory with blue outlines and features in madder and yellow. The most dominant feature, however, is the royal crown shown in the centre of the rug. This is finely delineated and takes the form of the familiar tri-lobed shape which is known from the 18th century and was particularly favoured by the Qajars. Such examples are seen in other art forms, notably in Qajar paintings. On this rug the crown is unusually prominent and forms part of a pattern extending outwards so that the other crowns to the side are seen slipping away under the border.

The main border has a series of stylised rosettes and palmettes enfolded by leaves. The palette is again a range of reds and blues on an ivory field. The guardbands are complex and comparatively wide and have to either side of the border an unusual feature in the form of square motifs with rosettes which recall architectonic features as seen guarding mouldings and friezes.

The rug is composed with a delightful degree of harmony and balance of design. Its quality should be no surprise in view of the fact that it probably had a royal original owner.

REFERENCES
For examples of Qajar paintings see Falk, op. cit.; cf. also plate 2.

STRUCTURE
size: 180 x 133 cm
weft: Silk, 2 strands
weft colour: Natural
warp: Silk, 2 strands
warp colour: Natural
side cords: Silk, new 1 strand
side cords colour: New madder
ends: Nil
knots: Symmetrical, short floss silk
dyes: Vegetable
knot count: 18 x 18 = 324 per sq in
total: 1,207,710

9 PERSIA
North West Persian Silk Medallion Rug

Late 19th Century

As with the previous examples of medallion rugs, this superb piece demonstrates yet a further variation on a seemingly endless creative theme.

The main field is of madder on which are a series of flowers and leaves in ivory, yellow and turquoise. There is a central medallion with pendants and extended corner pieces.

The main border has an ivory field on which are a series of red and indigo palmettes linked by tendrils. To either side of the border are the repeating guardbands composed of small rosettes and tendrils on madder. The narrow sub-guards have a barley sugar design. The imposing central medallion has an indigo field, whilst that of the pendants is in ivory. Floral devices, notably rosettes and palmettes, dominate, whilst the main medallion also has a large rosette centrally. About the flowers are a series of elegantly drawn leaves. The vegetal themes of the medallion are taken up in the corner pieces, likewise with an indigo field which extends around all sides of the main field.

The design of this fine example contains many elements which can be traced back to the exceptionally creative period of the 16th and 17th centuries. It is a testimony to the endurance of the tradition that the artists of the north west were able to take and develop such themes to produce the magnificent work shown here.

REFERENCES
See Wilber, D N, 'Heriz rugs', *Hali*, 1984, vol. 6, no. 21.

STRUCTURE
size: 186 x 134 cm
weft: Silk, 1 strand
weft colour: Red
warp: Silk, 2 strands
warp colour: Natural
side cords: Silk, 3 strands
side cords colour: Pale indigo
ends: Nil
knots: Symmetrical, short floss silk
dyes: Vegetable
knot count: 19 x 19 = 361 per sq in
total: 1,396,709

10 PERSIA
North West Persian Silk Medallion Rug

Early 20th Century

The overall themes of the other medallion rugs in the collection from this part of Persia are maintained here. However, the main central medallion has features which link it directly with major classical examples and it may indicate an attempt by the master craftsmen to re-invigorate their designs by taking inspiration from their forebears. This example is probably from Tabriz.

The main field is of madder with floral devices, flowers and scrolling tendrils which emanate from the central medallion and its extensions. These devices are mainly in ivory and various shades of blue.

The border of this rug is a wide and complex one. The main element has a series of palmettes and rosettes joined by tendrils, with the same themes repeated in the guardbands and also in the sub-guards. The palette is of ivory with the floral features in blues and red.

The main medallion is a complex one with eight lobes and a central rosette like a sunburst.

It is composed of ivory, indigo and madder. The form of this medallion would seem to owe its origins notably to those rugs known as Sanguszko. Such rugs are not only amongst the finest creations of the Safavid period, but at the period that this piece was produced were a source of inspiration to contemporary designers. The importance of the theme is also seen in rugs manufactured in Istanbul at approximately the same time (see below). In contrast to the Safavid precedent, the field of this work remains with only floral motifs and includes none of the animal or even human figures that might have been expected.

Whilst much of the work of north west Persia during the latter part of the 19th century and the early years of the present century show the natural development of traditional themes in design, this rug with its central medallion would appear to link directly with the classical precedents and it may be that the master designer concerned was influenced by such precedents as were available to him, or was familiar with the great exhibitions and associated catalogues of classical manufactures which became available from the middle of the 19th century onwards.

REFERENCES
See also plate 24 for a not dissimilar medallion.

STRUCTURE
size: 117 x 170 cm
weft: Silk, 2 strands
weft colour: Mixed colours
warp: Silk, 2 strands
warp colour: Mixed colours
side cords: Silk, 2 strands
side cords colour: Indigo
ends: Nil
knots: Symmetrical, short floss silk
dyes: Vegetable and chemical
knot count: 18 x 18 = 324 per sq in
total: 998,568

11 PERSIA
North West Persian Silk Medallion Rug

Late 19th Century

In contrast to the preceding medallion rugs in the collection, this superb work is most striking in its elegant geometricised apparent simplicity. Its links with earlier masterworks are less obvious and suggest an indigenous development in the north west of a particular artistic expression.

The main field is of a striking 'aubergine' on which is a main medallion, palmettes, and pendants with half medallions repeating at top and bottom. Above the indigo field of the medallion is a complex and stylised mass of blossoms. The main border is a series of scrolling leaves and blossoms in brown and ivory on an indigo field. The axes bear small blossoms in ivory, madder and turquoise. The guardbands contain small floral devices, whilst the whole rug is protected by a further outer subguard. The impact of the main medallions is enhanced by the series of spiked protrusions around the whole of the medallions which end in a fine delicate blossom. Around the whole field is a most unusual linear design with features incorporating a herringbone motif. From this feature, extending into the main field are a series of elegant blossoms in ivory.

The impact of this rug is most powerful, not only in terms of its unusual colouring but in the directness of the draughtsmanship to produce a unique and elegant effect.

STRUCTURE
size: 138 x 186 cm
weft: Silk, 2 strands
weft colour: Natural
warp: Silk, 2 strands
warp colour: Natural
side cords: Silk, 1 strand
side cords colour: Madder
ends: Nil
knots: Symmetrical, short floss silk
dyes: Vegetable
knot count: 20 x 20 = 400 per sq in
total: 1,576,800

12 PERSIA
North West Persian Multi Medallion Silk Rug

Late 19th Century

The centuries old tradition of north west Persia included a large contribution from the Armenian community whose traditional homelands straddled the border. There are many examples of the importance of the Armenians in weaving and rug manufacture during the medieval period, although in later ages they concentrated more on acting as important middlemen. Many of the ateliers of north west Persia were working for Armenian merchants and a number of items would certainly have been destined for the Armenian community itself. This strikingly beautiful rug with its prominent central cruciform feature may well be such an example.

The main field is of a deep burgundy of great power and originality. Upon this are a series of floral motifs with four magnificent medallions resting in the arms of the cruciform located centrally, which itself is part of a continuous design. The border contains a series of palmettes and leaves on an indigo field and is protected by complex triple guardbands.

The four medallions in the main field have indigo fields. They have eight lobes and contain a series of blossoms in yellow, red and blue with ivory palmettes and leaves around their central feature. The arms of the crosses are of indigo with blossoms and a central rosette utilising a palette of red, old gold and pistachio.

The colouring and design of this rug is almost unique. The prominent cruciform section makes an Armenian origin, or commission, most likely. The design is of a continuous type which extends *ad infinitum* so that the border acts as a frame enabling us to peer down on a part of this pattern. The importance of the Armenians during this period and their role in the trading of fine pieces has yet to be fully examined, but from this and other known examples their contribution is clearly a major and substantial one.

REFERENCES
For the use of Armenian Christian motifs such as cruciforms, etc., see der Manuelian, L, and Eiland, M L, *Weavers, Merchants and Kings*, Fort Worth, 1984, p. 36 et seq.

STRUCTURE
size: 130 x 224 cm
weft: Silk, 3 strands
weft colour: Natural
warp: Cotton, 3 strands
warp colour: Natural
side cords: Silk, 2 strands
side cords colour: Madder
ends: Nil
knots: Symmetrical, short floss silk
dyes: Vegetable and chemical
knot count: 18 x 18 = 324 per sq in
total: 1,470,636

13 PERSIA
North West Persian Silk Tree of Life Rug

Late 19th Century

Most of the finest silk examples produced in the area during the latter part of the 19th century concerned themselves with work in the format of prayer rugs and medallion rugs. There is, however, also a tradition incorporating the tree of life and numerous animal and 'futuristic' elements. This handsome piece is particularly interesting as it shows a development of the tree of life theme by incorporating a series of birds.

The main field is a glorious wine colour on which are depicted in old gold the tree of life with its branches, leaves and fruit. The most striking feature is the series of birds. The border has an old gold field with a series of wine-red tri-lobed blossoms, between which stand stylised cypress trees. The guardbands to either side contain blossoms and leaves in ivory on an indigo field.

The birds featured are most interesting. At the very top of the tree there appears to be a bird which might be an owl. Within the Persian tradition this bird is regarded as a creature of ruined places and may obliquely suggest the mortality of all living things. Below are a pair of hoopoes clearly identifiable by their crests which traditionally are associated with the Qur'anic references in which they are divine messengers, carrying messages between Solomon and the Queen of Sheba. The two birds at the base of the tree may represent partridges, which within the poetic tradition are noted for their graceful walk. Centrally in the guardband at the top of the piece is a commission number, 21.

Apart from the imagery associated with the tree of life and the birds, in the central field the artist has combined a restrained use of colour with a remarkable degree of exquisite draughtsmanship to produce a striking and important example of his art.

REFERENCES

The Qur'anic references to the hoopoe are associated with Solomon and Bilqis, the Queen of Sheba. See Qur'an, XXVII: 20 et seq.

STRUCTURE

size: 172 x 127 cm
weft: Silk, 2 strands
weft colour: Natural
warp: Silk, 2 strands
warp colour: Natural
side cords: Silk (new), 1 strand
side cords colour: New Beige
ends: Nil
knots: Symmetrical, short floss silk
dyes: Vegetable and chemical
knot count: 18 x 18 = 324 per sq in
total: 1,101,600

14 PERSIA
North West Persian Silk Rug

Early 20th Century

This very fine work is another example of the constant inventiveness of the masterweavers of north west Persia and the city of Tabriz.

The fine madder field carries an apparently complex design featuring strapwork and a host of blossoms and palmettes. The border has an indigo field with palmettes and sweeping leaves in an arabesque form in madder, ivory and light blue. The repeating guardbands to either side have a golden field and a design of small blossoms and scrolling tendrils.

The main design with indigo strapwork has highlights in gold and light blue. At the hand-like junctions are palmettes and blossoms. Also featured in the field are a series of blue cloudbands.

The artistic precedents for this work would seem to lie in the great classical pieces of the 17th century, where such lattice work and division into compartments became a feature of many Safavid masterpieces. There are also architectural parallels in the use of such designs in tile work and mosaic faience.

The artist has achieved a superb harmony of colour and design combined with great technical excellence. He has produced a work which again gives us a view of an infinitely extending pattern in which the observer may pause and contemplate.

REFERENCES

Similar classical examples are in the Metropolitan Museum of Art, New York (gift of Mrs Harry Payne Bingham), and the Museum für Kunst und Gewerbe, Hamburg.

STRUCTURE
size: 130 x 203 cm
weft: Silk, 3 strands
weft colour: Natural
warp: Silk, 2 strands
warp colour: Natural
side cords: Silk, 1 strand
side cords colour: Madder
ends: Nil
knots: Asymmetrical, short floss silk
dyes: Vegetable
knot count: 18 x 18 = 324 per sq in
total: 1,321,920

15 PERSIA
North West Persian Silk Vase Carpet

Early 20th Century

This is a magnificent example of the reviving north west Persian silk manufacturing tradition which responded to the demand for luxury goods by using traditional designs with traditional high standards of excellence, centred on Tabriz.

The main field of wine red bears a host of palmettes and blossoms whose stems run across the field to form lightly defined compartments.

In contrast with the main field, the border is indigo and carries large rosettes in red, white and silver, between which are sprays of flowers in ivory arranged in squares of sixteen. The guardbands to either side are of silver and adorned with rosettes and leaves.

The large blossoms in the main field use a palette of blue, indigo and ivory. Between them and their tendrils are a series of other small blossoms. There are a number of important Safavid precedents for this design which appears to derive from the vase design. Some authorities have associated it with Tabriz and it may be that the use of the design here is the natural re-interpretation of a local theme. The general design has also inspired other later work, both in Persia and Ottoman Turkey.

REFERENCES

There are a number of classical precedents for this lattice and palmette design, notably two examples in the Victoria and Albert Museum.

STRUCTURE

size: 140 x 203 cm
weft: Floss silk, 1 strand
weft colour: Pale blue
warp: Floss silk, 1 strand
warp colour: Natural
side cords: Silk, 1 strand
side cords colour: Madder
ends: Nil
knots: Symmetrical, long floss silk
dyes: Chemical
knot count: 18 x 18 = 324 per sq in
total: 1,425,600

16 PERSIA
Fine Woollen Tabriz Rug

Ascribed to masterweaver Haji Jalil

Late 19th Century

Although much of the most famous work of north west Persia from this period is in its magnificent silk creations, there does exist a number of superb wool examples from the same area and period. The magnificence of this piece would be more easily understood were it in fact in silk. Such is the quality and excellence of design that it has been associated with the name of Haji Jalil.

The main field is of a consistent pure ivory on which are four flowers, the main medallion and two half medallions.

The border with its indigo ground has a series of rosettes, somewhat stylised, embraced by leaves with smaller blossoms between in a palette principally of orange, red and blue. The complex guardbands to either side of the border have rosette features and leaves in indigo and madder. The unusual feature is the way in which the guardbands on the long axes are cut away to allow the corresponding points of the central medallion to approach the border at this point.

The diamond medallion and its half diamonds to either side have a large floral design in turquoise placed centrally with blossoms in white. The borders of the medallion have saw-teeth edges ending in a delicate hooked flowerhead. The field itself has an inner sub-guard of similar hooked flowers. The four flowers with their stylised blossoms, leaves and branches in ivory and madder extend into the plain ivory field.

This superb example has certain design features which may be compared with plate 11 above. It has been produced with the finest wool to an amazing degree of skill and technical excellence. The originality and impact of its elegant design and harmony of colour show great inventiveness.

STRUCTURE
size: 143 x 182 cm
weft: Cotton, 3 strands
weft colour: Natural
warp: Cotton, 3 strands
warp colour: Natural
side cords: Cotton, 2 strands
side cords colour: Natural but restored red
ends: Nil
knots: Symmetrical, short pile, wool
dyes: Vegetable and chemical
knot count: 20 x 20 = 400 per sq in
total: 1,612,800

17 PERSIA
North East Persian Silk Rug
19th Century

It is known from historical references that a number of manufacturers were active in the area of Khurasan during the 19th century. It had been an area of considerable importance in earlier times and is known to have been producing rugs and carpets during the period of the Safavids. Amongst these great cities was Herat which is now in Afghanistan. This particular example is probably from the Mashhad area and shows great originality and faithfulness to the traditions.

The technique of knotting used classes the work as *Turkbaf*, indicating it as the product of craftsmen/artists displaced from their homelands, a feature common throughout Persian history and which helps explain the many apparent anomalies of technique and design.

The main field is of a mellow ivory with a series of palmettes in subtle shades of orange and red arranged in rows. Between these rows of flowerheads are cloudband devices, mainly in indigo and madder. Centrally there is a square panel containing a hunting scene.

The border has a series of stylised rosettes with leaves in ivory, blue and gold on an indigo ground. The guardbands enclosing the border feature a simple scrolling device which is familiar from early architectural decoration, notably in the stucco work of the 11th century onwards.

The central panel is a striking and highly original feature. It has an indigo field containing a series of scattered blossoms. On the right-hand side is the figure of a hunter, who may be the traditional hero, Rustam, who is armed with a bow and assisted by his dogs in pursuing a gazelle. The figure has a full beard in the manner popular with early Qajars and wears a crown with wings which recalls that of the Sasanian monarchy.

The depiction of this intriguing scene centrally would derive from a long tradition, notably in painting and manuscript illustration. It is also not unknown for such scenes to be depicted on carpets and rugs.

During the 19th century there was a revival among the reigning Qajar dynasty of native Iranian traditions and, in particular, they showed an interest in the Sasanian dynasty which was that preceding the arrival of Islam in Persia. Just as this rug shows features deriving from Sasanian inspiration, the Qajars also created rock cut reliefs in the style of this ancient dynasty. There was also a revival of interest in the epic traditions of Persia. The scene shows a monarch engaged in one of the most popular and important pastimes, i.e. the hunt. At a time when so much of Persia's quality luxury output is from the north west of the country, the ability to create superb work in other areas is a reminder of the strength of the manufacturing tradition which the country possesses in a measure unequalled elsewhere.

REFERENCES

The Qajars were inspired by the pre-Islamic tradition of Iran and the scene shown centrally recalls a number of bas reliefs made by the Qajars after the manner of the Sasanians: for example, the reliefs at Shiraz and at Rayy.

STRUCTURE

size: 127 x 173 cm
weft: Silk, 3 strands
weft colour: Natural
warp: Silk, 2 strands
warp colour: Natural
side cords: Silk, 1 strand
side cords colour: Madder
ends: Nil
knots: Symmetrical, short floss silk
dyes: Vegetable
knot count: 14 x 14 = 196 per sq in
total: 666,400

18 PERSIA
Fine Woollen Doroksh

Late 19th Century

As with the previous example, this magnificent rug derives not from the north west of the country but from the north east, from an area of Khurasan somewhat to the south of the city of Mashhad. Although these areas were less productive than Azarbaijan, as these examples indicate, the quality they were able to produce is quite astonishing.

The main field of the rug is dominated by an orange madder. On this are a series of rows of regularly arranged botehs among a tight pattern of floral sprays.

The border carries a main design of blossoms in a diamond shape with stylised leaves in a range of reds and blues. The guardbands are composed of three narrow stripes with floral devices. The main design with its rows of botehs in reds and blues with the sprays of flowers between them make this a striking and powerful piece. The manufacturing area is one which suffered economic decline after the end of the Safavid period. However, the tradition was maintained. In part, this may be due to its relationship with the city of Kirman in the south east. Certainly this latter area maintained its rug manufacturing tradition aided in part by its ongoing textile industry. Indeed, many features of this rug recall the fine textiles of the south east which were so popular in Persia as well as the outside world.

REFERENCES
See Black, D, ed., *World Rugs and Carpets*, London, 1985, p. 154.

STRUCTURE
size: 251 x 163 cm
weft: Cotton, 3 strands
weft colour: Natural
warp: Cotton, 2 strands
warp colour: Natural
side cords: Wool, 1 strand
side cords colour: Madder
ends: Nil
knots: Asymmetrical, short wool
dyes: Vegetable
knot count: 25 x 25 = 625 per sq in
total: 4,120,000

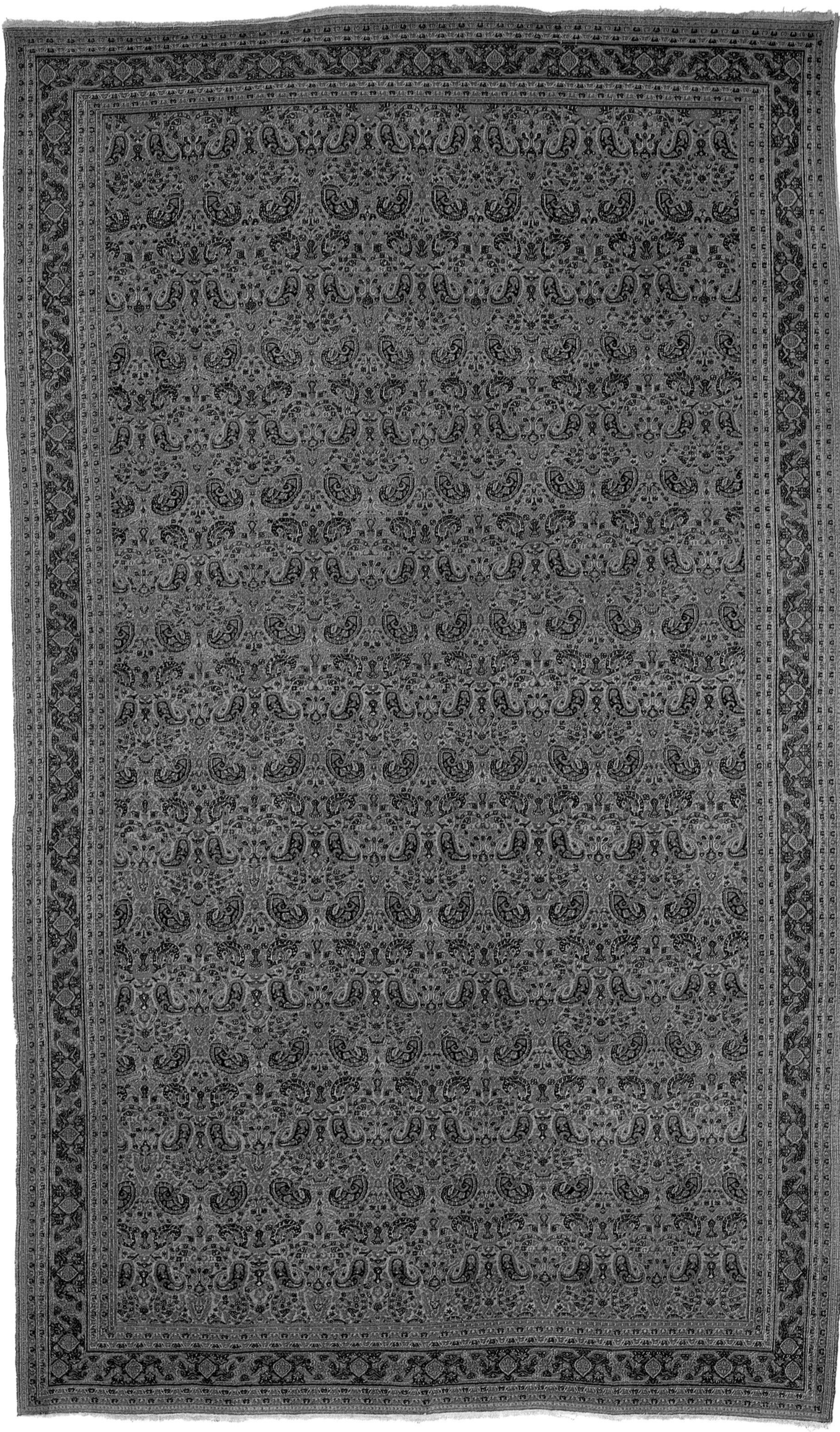

19 PERSIA
Fine Silk Ferahan Rug

Late 19th Century

Situated in western Persia, the area of Ferahan became an increasingly important area during the latter part of the 19th century. At this time it was also responsible for the manufacture of some beautiful and important silk rugs, as this example indicates.

The main field is of ivory filled with a range of blossoms and bearing a tree of life with a vase at the bottom. The main field also has a design recalling the shape of the mihrab.

The border has a series of palmettes enclosed by tendrils, giving the impression of a series of lozenges. Also prominent are groups of blossoms arranged in a cruciform shape. The field is of rose madder with design features in indigo, ivory and pistachio. The enclosing guardbands to either side of the border have a flowing scroll motif of leaves enclosing blossoms in rose madder, ivory and blue.

The main design carries in the upper part an arch form whose scalloped edge has become somewhat angular. This is carried through the sides of the main field down to the base. The edge of this frame has a design recalling a barley sugar or rope work.

Although superficially in the format of a prayer rug with a vase in the manner of many works from the north west of the country, this is a local adaptation of the design. As with many so called prayer rugs, its function was probably as a wall hanging and not for use as a prayer rug. The area of Ferahan was capable of producing work of the highest quality and this example re-enforces that view, with a refreshing and impressive design.

REFERENCES
See Edwards, op. cit., although little serious work has been done on the silk rugs of this area.

STRUCTURE
size: 132 x 206 cm
weft: Silk, 3 strands
weft colour: Pale red
warp: Silk, 3 strands
warp colour: Natural
side cords: Silk, 1 strand
side cords colour: Madder
ends: Wide band ends of madder colour
knots: Symmetrical, short floss silk
dyes: Vegetable
knot count: 14 x 14 = 196 per sq in
total: 825,552

20 TURKEY
Silk and Metal Thread Rug, Istanbul

Late 19th Century

From about 1870 onwards the masterweavers of Istanbul began to take up traditional themes from the great classical works of the 17th century to re-invigorate the carpet manufacturing tradition. This magnificent work indicates the degree to which they were able to adapt ancient design features, especially the precedent of 'polonais' rugs, which were mainly created as regal gifts, and ally them to an exceptionally high technical excellence.

The knotting employed is asymmetrical which may indicate that it is the work of immigrant Persian masters, or that it is a conscious attempt to echo the polonais in technique as well as design.

This rug is made most memorable by the amount of metal thread employed on the main field. The field also carries a large multi-lobed medallion featuring fighting monsters, with corner pieces, and the open area of the field also filled with animals, flowers and tendrils. The border contains large palmettes joined by the great, sweeping, wide leaves in ivory and blue which also have 16th and 17th century precedents. The guardbands contain small blossoms and leaves.

In the main field is the familiar symbol of the lion fighting with a bull. Other beasts of the chase are seen amongst the plants. The pistachio field of the central medallion carries a large entwining serpent fighting another mystical beast among blossoms. The matching corner pieces, also with a pistachio field, depict birds as well as flowers.

This extraordinary work contains precedents from the classical period for its borders as well as in the animals featured in the main field. The dragon shown centrally may well derive from the epic tradition of the area in which the literary precedent of Persia was most important. A not dissimilar design also exists in an example held by a private collector in the UK. The manufacturers of Istanbul, and in due course those of Kumkapı, re-invigorated their tradition by using classical examples. Not only were these available to them as a result of those works seen by masterweavers in and around the many Turkish palaces, but classical masterworks also became available through the great European collections by way of exhibitions and catalogues. The powerful design here achieved is enhanced by the continuation of its important design motifs produced to a high degree of technical excellence.

REFERENCES

For current attitudes to Polonais rugs see *The Eastern Carpet in the Western World*, pp. 29, 69; see also Bensoussan, P, 'The Masterweavers of Istanbul', *Hali*, 1985, no. 26.

STRUCTURE

size: 190 x 130 cm
weft: Silk, 3 strands
weft colour: Natural
warp: Silk, 3 strands
warp colour: Natural
side cords: Silk, 4 strands
side cords colour: Pale blue
ends: Nil
knots: Asymmetrical, short floss silk and metal
dyes:
knot count: 20 x 20 = 400 per sq in
total: 1,530,000

21 TURKEY
Silk Hereke Rug

Late 19th/early 20th Century

The Imperial workshops of Hereke and those established in the Istanbul area provided not only a source of superb works for the Ottoman court but, in due course, also began to supply the demand for luxury goods in outside markets. Hence the amazing technical excellence of the area was responsible for this magnificent example.

The main field has a pale powder blue ground and is filled with a scene of trees, plants and animals which depicts either an earthly or a celestial paradise.

The main border has a claret field with rose cloudbands, blue palmettes and ivory tendrils. The inner guardband has a series of small blossoms whilst the outer one, which is also wider, has a claret field with stylised blossoms and small human faces and birds joined by ivory tendrils.

The main design has trees, notably the cypress and willows. The former is frequently found as an image of the beauty of the beloved, whilst the willows are trees traditionally linked to the suffering of the lover, and that of Majnun for Layla in particular. Also featured are a series of animals which include lions, hares, gazelles and more exotic beasts. The many and varied blossoms depicted are in a range of browns, greens and pinks.

Apart from the many traditional elements familiar from the many centuries of carpet manufacturing, this rug is an example of the way in which allusions from other artistic traditions such as literature are important for understanding better the imagery of such work. Not only is there the significance of the trees, the animals and a garden scene recalling paradise, but even the human faces in the outer guardband recall the old legend of the waq-waq tree which bore talking heads.

In this magnificent work the artist has brought together a series of allusions and themes which prove an endless source of delight and stimulation and which demonstrates, when allied to its technical excellence, the power of manufacturing in Istanbul at this period.

REFERENCES
See Bensoussan, op. cit.

STRUCTURE
size: 151 x 221 cm
weft: Floss silk, 1 strand
weft colour: Blue
warp: Silk, 4 strands
warp colour: Natural
side cords: Silk, 4 strands
side cords colour: Pale blue
ends: Pale blue band with red line
knots: Symmetrical, short floss silk
dyes: Vegetable
knot count: 22 x 22 = 484 per sq in
total: 2,526,480

22 TURKEY
Istanbul Silk Tree of Life Rug
Late 19th/early 20th Century

The main theme in this superb work is again that of the tree of life within the paradisal garden. The masterweavers of Istanbul and the adjacent areas were constantly developing the traditional themes and classical precedents. Interestingly in this fine work the artist has chosen a more naturalistic and self-expressive design incorporating the traditional themes.

The main field is one of a magnificent wine red. On this is depicted the tree of life surrounded by various blossoms and a range of birdlife.

The border has a grey-green field with flowerheads and leaves in ivory, madder and indigo. The guardbands differ, although both have elements containing flowerheads and leaves utilising a range of colours dominated by green, indigo and madder.

The design of the main field has rendered the tree of life in yellow with principally ivory blossoms. Among the other flowers in the main field are palmettes and naturalistic roses. Many of the birds featured are aquatic, such as cranes or herons and other wading birds. Others featured include what appear to be partridges (cf. plate 13), forest fowl of the chase and a superb peacock with open tail created with a remarkable degree of precision.

The very natural way in which this composition has been created shows an individual approach on the part of the artist in which he has depicted a series of classical elements. He is thereby reflecting the constant development of the old form and indicates here elements of change which are influenced by Western attitudes and norms.

REFERENCES
See Bensoussan, op. cit.

STRUCTURE
size: 203 x 140 cm
weft: Floss silk, 1 strand
weft colour: Natural
warp: Silk, 3 strands
warp colour: Natural
side cords: Silk, 1 strand
side cords colour: Beige
ends: Nil
knots: Symmetrical, long floss silk
dyes: Vegetable and chemical
knot count: 28 x 28 = 784 per sq in
total: 3,449,600

23 TURKEY
Istanbul Silk Rug

Early 20th Century

This handsome and very beautiful example is probably the work of the exceptional group of masters of Armenian background who were working mainly under royal patronage in the years before the First World War and, in some cases, just after. Dominated by the mastery of Zareh, this group of Kumkapı masters achieved an unsurpassed degree of technical ability allied to the inspiration of 16th and 17th century classical designs.

The main field of this rug is a wine red on which are a series of palmettes joined by a delicate lattice of tendrils with smaller palmettes interspersed, blossoms, cloudbands and pairs of birds.

The border has an indigo field on which are a series of beautifully drawn palmettes joined by leaves and tendrils which scroll to form restrained arabesques. These features are created in gold, madder and ivory. The inner narrower guardband has a gold field with small blossoms and tendrils, whilst the wider outer one has small palmettes and stylised leaves in madder.

The main design with its delicate lattice, palmettes, birds and cloudbands has a palette principally using golds, pistachio and indigo. The design itself would seem to be linked to the great series of carpets believed to have originated in eastern Persia during the Safavid period, and it is well known that the masters of Istanbul had access to such work through important exhibitions and examples in the various and numerous palaces of the capital city. Such sources of inspiration for design were allied to the remarkable technical excellence that was achieved by not only painstaking care and attention, but also by a thorough knowledge of the classical techniques. Such exceptional work probably forms part of the swan song of the last great period of oriental carpet manufacturing.

REFERENCES

See Bensoussan, op. cit. The classical precedents derived from the group of rugs from 16th century Persia usually ascribed to Herat, for example, the work in the Thyssen-Bornemisza collection of oriental rugs.

STRUCTURE

size: 129 x 190 cm
weft: Silk, 2 strands
weft colour: Natural
warp: Silk, 3 strands
warp colour: Natural
side cords: Silk, 3 strands
side cords colour: Green
ends: Nil
knots: Symmetrical, short floss silk
dyes: Vegetable and chemical
knot count: 23 x 23 = 529 per sq in
total: 2,023,425

24 TURKEY
Fine Silk Istanbul Rug

Early 20th Century

This beautiful jewel-like example contains a series of elements and quality of technique which point to the Istanbul area in the great manufacturing period around the time of the First World War. As with the previous example, and in conformity with contemporary ateliers, it owes a debt to many classical features.

The main field, dominated by a wine red, has a superb multi-lobed medallion with pendants and corner pieces, whilst the field has a series of scenes from the chase.

The border has a number of figures representing angels with gifts who are brought together by a flowing delicate arabesque interspersed with small palmettes. The matching guardbands have small blossoms joined by tendrils.

This work contains many classical features. There are a number of small aquatic birds, probably ducks, featured which some authorities believe have a symbolic meaning. Further, the elements within the magnificent medallion and corner pieces both suggest a form of the great band motif but are effectively the sinuous bodies of serpents. The use of medallions, corner pieces and the field of hunters and animals suggests a link with the so-called Sanguszko group of Safavid rugs which are now located in a number of international museums (see above, plate 10). The angels within the borders also have 16th century precedents, notably in the great carpets formerly the property of the Hapsburgs. There are also manuscript parallels for the use of such figures.

The remarkable degree of excellence in terms of design and technique emphasises the special position of these masterweavers in Istanbul.

REFERENCES

See Bensoussan, op. cit. The main classical precedents for the border and the Sanguszko design of the field derive from Safavid examples, as that illustrated in Trenkwald, H, and Sarre, F, *Old Oriental Carpets*, Vienna and Leipzig, 1926, vol. 1. The angels are also familiar in 16th century examples in the Victoria and Albert Museum, London, and the Musée Historique des Tissus, Lyon.

STRUCTURE

size: 127 x 188 cm
weft: Silk, 2 strands
weft colour: Natural
warp: Silk, 3 strands
warp colour: Red
side cords: Silk, 1 strand
side cords colour: Red
ends: Plain red band
knots: Symmetrical, long floss silk
dyes: Vegetable and chemical
knot count: 20 x 20 = 400 per sq in
total: 1,598,400

CHAPTER SEVEN

THE FUNCTION OF SYMBOL

THE turbulent historical setting of the rugs shown in this book is not reflected in their tranquil and harmonious ambience. The important themes of design emphasise the garden, and hence paradise, which is part of the Islamic and Turko-Persian regal tradition. Whether, as has been suggested,[1] we can associate design elements with particular intentions would seem an area worthy of much greater study and in which a close acquaintance with the manufacturing areas, their history, society and artistic tradition, is called for.

Art is irrevocably linked with the symbol: symbols as the cohesive elements in a work of art, the work of art itself as a symbol and the overall concept of art as a symbol-making process. Exploring the layers of meaning is as complex as investigating the structure of human thought and language. To pretend therefore that the elements of design in oriental rugs can be simply evaluated in their symbolic terms is misleading. The problem is compounded by the need to describe one symbolic system in terms of another – that is, the pictorial in terms of the linguistic. How much more difficult when we are also dealing with a shift in that linguistic spectrum, from Persian through Turkish to English and back, providing terms that cannot easily be equated.

Symbols at certain times are 'active' within people's minds, and at other times remain 'at rest'.[2] When active, symbols frequently shift meaning – people elaborate on symbols and create something from themselves which is projected onto those symbols. Cultural and religious symbols will generally engage people in an attempt to identify what is specific to their culture. Some people, however, are, or profess to be, 'symbolblind', that is they simply take the image at its surface value; others elaborate whole worlds out of symbols. The depth of elaboration would seem dependent on the use to which an image or work of art was being put. Choosing not to see the ramifications of an image may serve a particular social or political purpose; elaborating the image may serve otherwise.

It is the individual purpose of elaboration which causes difficulties in the world of the oriental rug. Problematical here is of course the varied responses of different cultures: it may be quite valid, say, for a Western scholar to elaborate on the symbols to be found within a rug, but the implications to an Eastern scholar may be totally different. Divisions within Eastern society similarly cause a difference in interpretation between religious sects and the users of the rug, between designer and weavers. Interpretation is then dependent on the overall intent of the commentator.

Symbols are used by groups in relations with each other[3] and therefore acquire different meanings according to the group power structures: ' . . . no interpretation of a religious symbol can be called correct when it does not take into account all these different aspects: the literal meaning and the immediate cultural context; the social dimension and the structural position of the symbol within power relations; the latent associative aspects connected with feeling and emotion; some basic philosophical questions, in particular with regard to the existential problem(s) for which the symbol offers a kind of solution.'[4]

☆   ☆   ☆

From what do we derive the need for symbols? Jung and the school of psychologists who followed him in Europe made this need a cornerstone of their theoretical approach. Jung himself divided the human mind into several elements: the conscious and unconscious, the introvert and extrovert, the personal unconscious and the collective unconscious. He construed symbol and its narrative counterpart, myth, as the connection between the elements of consciousness.

In Jungian theory, myths and the manipulation of symbols are seen as ways of adapting to the world. The myth, that is, the delusional system, is not simply a way of escaping reality, but of dealing with it. Everybody lives by myths, giving themselves a dignity and purpose in life. Religion, through folklore, to schizophrenia are all myth-creating phases along a continuum. In Waardenburg's terms, symbols, especially religious ones, transpose people to another reality. Religion is simply a network of symbols which raises questions of meaning and seems to provide possible answers, thus making life bearable.

Along this myth-continuum, at its various points, are employed symbols, both visual and linguistic, which directly relate to the notions of dignity and purpose. Thus we encounter images of the egg, the jewel, the flower, and ball, all representative, in Jung's perspective, of the self. Similarly, geometric figures such as the square and the equal-armed cross are linked with the self and the concept of divine harmony (see plate 12). This is particularly true of all concentrically arranged figures like the mandala – radial or spherical – (see, for example, plates 6 and 11) and those images containing four-fold elements, which represent powerful symbols of wholeness. This kind of symbol is of very ancient origin and includes the fylfot, which is often to be found on rugs and tribal pieces, as well as the circle.

The importance of these symbols to Jung was

Pattern detail of an arch from the ruined mosque at Farumad, 13th century, Khurasan, Persia.

involved with the self-regulating psyche. The divisions of consciousness create a need for the balance and harmony of opposites. It is the psyche which seeks this balance between the forces at work within the individual.

The all-important concept of the collective unconscious Jung defined as the myth-making part of the mind which is common to all cultures, as language is common to all cultures. This is evidenced by the fact that similar myths are created in cultures which have no apparent connection and Jung saw this stemming from the fact that there are certain processes which are common to all human beings at all times. For example, emancipation from one's parents and establishing one's own place in life is a process common to every culture. It is not surprising then to discover the existence of 'hero' myths, which describe this process symbolically, existing in every culture. We may have such an example in the depiction of a hero on plate 17, echoing the story of Rustam, one of the greatest figures in the hero mythology of Persia. In the same way, common symbols, such as the circle and the cross, have an existence within the collective unconscious and occur throughout the world.

The symbol and myth-making processes are manifested in dreams, in art and all systems of abstraction, including language and meaning. It is by these processes that human beings come to terms with the world. Not only do they reflect certain facets of reality but they enable also that reality to be grasped in such a way that the possibility of balance is arrived at. Jung saw the balance of opposites and its achievement as an essential need for the wholeness of human beings. This process can be seen in the fine symmetry of many rugs. The contemplation of balanced opposites, as in the arabesque, the harmony of colours or the balance of shape between medallions and borders, may be construed as a path towards divine grace. Central to this is the concept of the garden and paradise which combines both earthly and divine motifs and by a contemplation of the spiritual may lead to a reassessment of the imperfect, carnal world in which we live.

One of the commentators upon Jung's work, Anthony Storr, suggests that a human's adaptation to the material world is partially abstract and in order to motivate this abstraction, to achieve an essential wholeness, the human being develops an inner world of fantasy. It is precisely from this inner world of fantasy and abstract motivation that art emanates: 'A work of art is a true symbol in the Jungian sense, in that it is pregnant with meaning, partakes of both "conscious" and "unconscious", yet cannot be sharply defined in purely intellectual terms.'[5]

The collective unconscious also represents a pool of divine images – something in which God resides – in the sense that it is the spur to all religion. Like the Islamic concept (Jung's father was by no extraordinary coincidence a pastor and oriental scholar), creative people, artists of all kinds, exist as vessels to be filled by these divine images or messages.

Contrasting with this Jungian and Western perspective on symbols is the Islamic perspective. It is not true to say that Jung and others in the West ignore the notion of universality – the collective unconscious is after all based on such a concept – but there is nevertheless a strong element of the individual consciousness to be found within Jung's theories. Religion itself tends to be seen by many Western thinkers as a function of the individual psyche operating within the collective unconscious. Some Islamic philosophers may move towards the same point but from a totally different direction. Their ideas spring from the divine source and trace it down to the many facets of individualism.

For Eastern interpreters the symbol, like nature, is an expression of a religious concept. The principle of gnosis (the secret, initiated access to spiritual truths) governs Islamic art and is referred to as *Tariqah* (the Way). Unlike in the West, in Islamic art there is no distinction made between science and craft. Craft is the tangible product of scientific laws which themselves derive from metaphysical truths. All these elements manifest themselves in the guilds, which have been traditionally headed by a Sufi-craftsman, initiated into a *Tariqah*. We still await clarification of the rug manufactories and their involvement in mystic brotherhoods. However, of their importance in Turkey and Persia there is no doubt.

The teaching of the *Tariqah* implies that there is an external and an internal meaning to every thing – meanings available to both the 'symbol-blind' and the 'symbol-aware'. There is an obvious meaning available to the senses and one which denotes the qualitative, spiritual dimension. In both cases these manifestations lead back to the Divine.

Whether or not human beings choose to see it, whether they are initiated into the Way or not, all phenomena nevertheless possess symbolic significance. It is humankind's duty to reach the Truth within things, since its intellect relates to the Universal Intellect, and its being to the Pure Being. Only through the interpretation and pursuit of truth can unity with the Divine Source be achieved.

According to this interpretation, symbols reflect the knowledge gained through gnosis so that they are at once the key to and the manifestation of that knowledge: 'A symbol is a "reflection" in a lower order of existence of a reality belonging to a higher ontological status, a "reflection" which in essence is unified to that which is symbolized, . . .'[6]

Some interpreters attempt to classify symbols in various ways.[7] There is first the 'natural' symbol which is manifested in rhythmical and symmetrical systems, and expresses the 'inexhaustible multiplicity of creation' and the unity which is to be found therein. Such symbols would include the recurring pattern – the arabesque, the ever-repeating medallions which are seen, as it were, through a trapdoor onto infinity. Then there are symbols which are 'sanctified' by various traditions in the world: they may occur in various forms and languages and include numeric, calligraphic and linguistic symbols, perhaps in Jungian terms those symbols most readily to be found within the collective unconscious. Like natural symbols they manifest 'multiplicity within unity'.

In fact, the route to understanding the Islamic doctrine of symbol, according to some commentators using the vocabulary familiar within the Sufi tradition, lies in penetrating the term 'multiplicity within unity'. 'Unity' is the origin of 'multiplicity', the source of the temporary and the eternal, of flux and stasis. It is the immutable essence of things whose outward forms may nevertheless constantly change.[8] The symbol is a unique reflection of this quality, and the art form is its 'container'. As such the symbol possesses inner and outer meanings. If we take the arabesque, for example, it can be seen to reflect the multiplicity and flux of movement occurring on a static base, yet the moving shape itself partakes of unity and stasis: 'Symbols themselves are theophanies of the absolute in the relative.'[9]

There are certain Western scholars who for their own purposes have chosen to elaborate on the importance of symbol in the oriental rug by reference to the variety of cultures which may have provided input to that art form. The interpretations they make may or may not be appropriate. Symbols they enumerate include the border as sky-door, animals engaged in combat as the destruction of vanity and an expression of verbal puns, the garden as representative of paradise and botehs as tears from the tree of life.

However much our Western culture may wish to pin down meanings with what we call objective scientific precision, the concept of 'multiplicity' does at least accommodate multifarious facets of meaning as being a manifestation of the spiritual centre. Thus for one initiated into the Way, space-filling patterns, as exemplified on rugs, may express the 'multiplicity within unity', whereas an outsider's interpretation may simply ascribe space-filling to a cultural predilection for intricacy, colour and symmetry. Whether this springs from a need to offset the monotony of landscape or as a reflection of a complex, hierarchical society, or as an expression of an innermost truth is open to interpretation.

In any consideration of oriental rugs we should be aware of the multiplicity of approaches. It might be easy to assert that the depiction of a carnivore devouring its prey was representative in the masterweaver's mind of the destruction of vanity. Are we clear, though, that this idea stemmed from the skilled worker? Or the designer? Were any of those involved in the creation of the rug initiated into the mystical truths? It is less arduous to demonstrate the use of such a symbol within the Sufi literary tradition, but can we maintain with any certainty that similar ideas were current in the art of rug making? Only the similarity in bookbinding design or in architectural pattern can be pointed to.

Some of these questions may be more readily resolved if it could be proved conclusively that the manufacturers belonged to a guild with a local Sufi tradition. Even then, we could not be sure that the images were woven in anything other than a blind adherence to tradition. Many masterweavers today, for example, when asked for the names of particular flowers or symbols on the rugs can usually answer nothing more than 'flower'. Following Jungian theories, of course, the images might easily be construed as conjured from the collective unconscious, or from half-recognised meanings within a sea of images current in that particular society.

In the final analysis then, does it matter if Western admirers or scholars construct their own elaborations of meaning for the symbols and rugs? Like all works of art, like all symbols, they can be readily adapted to fit the relationships of interpretation and meaning, of power and strategy, that exist between groups in the society which uses them. Perhaps it is a loss that the original intentions of the creators, if there were any, are neglected, but like language and all forms of myth, the pictorial symbol is dynamic and will proliferate meaning for as long as it exists.

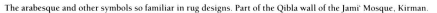

The arabesque and other symbols so familiar in rug designs. Part of the Qibla wall of the Jami' Mosque, Kirman.

The shrine of Shaykh Ni'matallah at Mahan, a garden within an arid landscape.

NOTES

1 See Cammann, S, 'Symbolic Meanings in Oriental Rug Patterns', *The Textile Museum Journal*, 111/3, December 1972.

2 Waardenburg, J, 'Symbolic Aspects of Myth', *Myth, Symbol and Reality*, ed. A M Olson, Notre Dame (Ind), 1980, p. 41.

3 Waardenburg, op. cit., p. 50.

4 Waardenburg, op. cit., p. 52.

5 Storr, A, *Jung*, London, 1973, pp. 112-113.

6 Nasr, S H, *Introduction to Islamic Cosmological Doctrines*, London, 1976, p. 263.

7 Ardalan, N, and Bakhtiar, L, *The Sense of Unity*, Chicago, 1973, p. 5 et seq.

8 Nasr, S H, *The Encounter of Man and Nature, the Spiritual Crisis of Modern Man*, London, 1968, p. 74 et seq.

9 Ardalan and Bakhtiar, op. cit., p. 5.

CHAPTER EIGHT
THE EAST IN WESTERN METAPHOR

FROM Renaissance times, the opulence of the East, where textiles and the finest rugs figure strongly, had been much admired. Writers in northern Europe, most of whom had no particular experience of travel in Eastern countries and had ventured no further afield than Italy, if anywhere, associated the area with the source of riches. This was not surprising since many of Europe's luxury goods, such as spices and fabrics, were Eastern imports. Thus, the rich lifestyles of the East, often grossly inflated, were the subject of much envy for Europeans, and writers, especially those given to the rhetorical hyperbole current in the English Renaissance, added to the impression. It was a land of adventure and distraction for many dramatists, full of brilliant caricatures, as Christopher Marlowe demonstrates in *The Jew of Malta*:

The wealthy Moor that in the eastern rocks
Without control can pick his riches up,
And in his house heap pearls like pebble stones . . .
Bags of fiery opals, sapphires, amethysts,
Jacinths, hard topaz, grass-green emeralds,
Beauteous rubies, sparkling diamonds,
And seld-seen costly stones of so great price.[1]

Marlowe, in fact, was one of the few writers who had a reasonable knowledge of the East. He had almost certainly read a copy of the work by Baptista Egnatius on the origin of the Turks.[2] Within his lifetime, however, the rich living of a certain limited section of the East's population and particularly the power of its rulers was no exaggeration – from 1520 was the age of Süleyman the Magnificent, followed by Selim II in 1566 and then Murat III from 1574-1595 – although their lifestyles were elaborated by hearsay and given an Elizabethan slant. The destitution and oppression of other sections of the Eastern population were, however, obliquely recognised, but only as a measure of a conqueror's tyranny:

With naked negroes shall thy coach be drawn,
And as thou rid'st in triumph through the streets
The pavement underneath thy chariot wheels
With Turkey carpets shall be covered
And cloth of Arras hung about the walls.[3]

It was not only the opulence of material goods which would have wielded an attraction for the Renaissance audience but also the opulence of slaughter. However untrue, the enormous cruelty of 'Tamburlaine' certainly provided great entertainment and the idea of the cruel and barbarous Eastern ruler, in spite or perhaps because of his magnificent living, was firmly planted in the Western mind. It was a propaganda motif which continued to be fed down the ages. That the condition of the lower classes within England and Europe at that time probably varied little from those in the East seems to have had no important impact on the newly ascendant bourgeoisie or the rulers of the West.

The oriental carpet, which began flooding into Europe at that time,[4] was seen as an essential part of the Eastern lifestyle. It was deemed synonymous with opulence, relaxation and leisure amidst natural beauty and became a prime focus for the nouveau riche as a tangible symbol of wealth. Not least was it also symbolic of the imagination, of sensual enjoyment, freedom and verdant nature.

Content, but we will leave this paltry land,
And sail from hence to Greece, to lovely Greece.
I'll be thy Jason, thou my golden fleece:
Where painted carpets o'er the meads are hurled,
And Bacchus' vineyards overspread the world:
Where woods and forests go in goodly green.[5]

It was this theme which continued down to the Western Romantic period, though much of the imagined opulence and power of the East was retrospective. Already Ottoman Turkey and Qajar Persia were losing ground in their struggle against Western expansionism. The reports which were being fed back by the increasing number of Western travellers (Lady Mary Wortley Montagu had written her famous series of letters between 1708 and 1720[6]) simply served to fuel the public imagination with images of riches and despotism. Coupled with recent translations of Eastern classics such as *The Thousand and One Nights*[7] these brilliant images were used by writers to break the bounds of previous restraints imposed by the Age of Reason and set their imaginations free. That the West, with its 'dark, satanic mills', was now the focus of power had not yet permeated, or was irrelevant to, the reading public's consciousness. The East was still the rich source of imported luxuries, to be plundered if necessary:

Manna and dates, in argosy transferred
From Fez; and spicèd dainties, every one,
From silken Samarcand to cedared Lebanon.[8]

Carpets along with other rich ornaments are frequently described as aspects of interior decoration, obviously reflecting as much the increasing use of such artefacts in the West as an understanding of Eastern lifestyles.

Haidée and Juan carpeted their feet
On Crimson satin, border'd with pale blue;
Their sofa occupied three parts complete
Of the apartment – and appear'd quite new;
The velvet cushions (for a throne more meet)
Were scarlet, from whose glowing centre grew
A sun emboss'd in gold, whose rays of tissue,
Meridian-like, were seen all light to issue.[9]

As in the Renaissance period, it was very much the upper class which was the central focus and any lesser mortals within Eastern society were usually mere subjects of oppression. This, of course, reflected the preoccupations in the West, where literacy was confined to the middle and upper classes and where, to all but a few like Shelley, the working masses were not the subject of any great regard. Thus few glimpses of an Eastern society in toto were provided. Many writers were simply inspired by stories from *The Thousand and One Nights* and the reports of travellers like Montagu, and had never been to the East. The consequent impression is much more one of a distortion of the East in a Western cultural mirror than of any factual account.

The elaborate and magnificent stucco carving on the mihrab of Uljaytu, 1310, Jami' Mosque, Isfahan.

Indeed, many of the settings could well have been inspired by the writers' view of interior decorations fashionable at that time in the West.[10] Their inspiration extended to the close links between carpets and natural surroundings, both in decoration and use:

They kissed nine times the carpet's velvet face
Of glossy silk, soft, smooth, and meadow-green,
Where the close eye in deep rich fur might trace
A silver tissue, scantily to be seen,
As daisies lurked in June-grass, buds in treen.[11]

The aspect of subservience attributed to the sultan's subjects in this verse touches upon one of the fascinations the East held for Western observers. This fascination, however, was tempered by a certain distaste for its tyrannical social structure as opposed to the more democratic tradition, extending only as far as the middle classes, of course, of the West. Such was the inspiration for Byron's participation in the Greek war of independence. This dual attitude is taken up in Beckford's *Vathek*[12] where the 'fantastic' tale and the tyrannous Eastern court are interwoven in a sparkling tapestry. Beckford's involvement with Eastern settings may well have stemmed from his visit to Spain.[13]

Much of the information gained by these writers, although Byron was an exception, came from writers like Montagu who, in the second decade of the 18th century, had had the privilege of residing in Turkey as wife of the British Ambassador. Her reports mainly centred on upper class lifestyle. Like many of her Western contemporaries the life of poorer sections of the populace, except those servants with whom she came in contact, were either kept from her or were of no significance to her. Consequently traders and artisans do not figure in her descriptions, much to the dismay of those looking for any descriptions of rug production. Despite her class insularity, her openness to other cultures is immediately apparent. Uses of the artisans' products and their place in upper class social niceties and lifestyle, especially amongst women, are liberally described. Some of the activities she indulged in, however, affected a wider stratum of society, like her visit to the public bath in Adrianople.

'I beleive [sic] in the whole there were 200 Women and yet none of those disdainfull smiles or satyric whispers that never fail in our assemblys when any body appears that is not dress'd exactly in fashion. . . The first sofas were cover'd with Cushions and rich Carpets, on which sat the Ladys, and on the 2nd their slaves behind 'em, but without any distinction of rank by their dress, all being in the state of nature, that is, in plain English, stark naked, without any Beauty or deffect conceal'd, yet there was not the least wanton smile or immodest Gesture amongst 'em. . .'[14]

This description inspired Ingres, who like many of the European writers had never been to Turkey, to artistic excellence in his painting of *Le Bain Turc*, which now hangs in the Louvre. Once again in Montagu's writing we have the focus fixed on interiors and their richness, although, given the restrictions placed on women, this is not so surprising. Such narrow focus on drawing room manners in any event occurs even a century later in England, in the novels of Jane Austen, for instance. Here she gives a description of the interior of her house in Adrianople, liberally decorated with carpets and embroidery, and castigates those writers who presume to describe without having visited:

'The rooms are all spread with Persian Carpets and rais'd at one end of 'em (my chamber is rais'd at both ends) about 2 foot. This is the Sopha and is laid with a richer sort of Carpet, and all round it a sort of Couch rais'd halfe a foot, cover'd with rich Silk according to the fancy or magnificence of the Owner. Mine is of Scarlet Cloath with a gold fringe. Round this are plac'd, standing against the Wall, 2 rows of Cushions, the first very large and the next little ones, and here the Turks display their greatest Magnificence. They are gennerally Brocade or embroidery of Gold Wire upon Satin. . . but what pleases me best is the fashion of having marble Fountains in the lower part of the room which throws up several spouts of Water, giving at the same time an agreable Coolness and a pleasant dashing sound falling from one basin to

another. . . You will perhaps be surpriz'd at an Account so different from what you have been entertaind with by the common Voyage-writers who are very fond of speaking of what they don't know.'[15]

Like Turkish upper class women Lady Wortley Montagu did at least partake of occasional excursions. In this manner she witnesses the favourite Turkish way of enjoying the countryside which is still today prevalent amongst Turks and other Eastern societies. Carpets in fact prove to be the most important artefact in this activity.

'The Summer is allready far advanc'd in this part of the World, and for some miles round Adrianople the whole ground is laid out in Gardens, and the Banks of the River set with Rows of Fruit trees, under which all the most considerable Turks divert themselves every Evening; not with walking, that is not one of their Pleasures, but a set party of 'em chuse out a green spot where the Shade is very thick, and there they spread a carpet on which they sit drinking their Coffée and generally attended by some slave with fine voice or that plays on some instrument.'[16]

After Montagu and particularly by the time of the Romantics, more and more travellers were journeying to the East not only for diplomatic and business reasons but also as part of an extended Grand Tour. Many brought with them their own prejudices. We may think that the English insularity abroad, the 'fish and chips in Spain' mentality, is only part of a recent phenomenon with the advent of travel for the working classes, but many upper class travellers in the 19th century exhibited just as much English snobbery and refusal to accept foreign cultures.[17]

In contrast, Théophile Gautier exemplifies the tradition of the later century, especially the French tradition, when realistic observation played such an important role in creative literature and was consequently reflected in the style of notebooks and journals. The general thrust of his book *Constantinople of To-day* is still centred on the lifestyle of the upper and middle classes, although views of ordinary people and the manufacturing processes are given, but much of this narrowness is understandably to do with access. One of the most interesting passages relates to silk production in Istanbul, not far from the Topkapı palace:

'At some distance from the Atmeidan, in the midst of a spot strewn with the ashes of former fires, and at the back of a hillock, gapes, like a great black mouth, the entrance of a gigantic Byzantine cistern. The descent is by a wooden staircase. The Turks call it Ben-Bir-

Dereck , or the Thousand-and-one Columns, although there are, in fact, but two hundred and twenty-four pillars. These columns, of white marble, are surmounted by large capitals, of a barbarous Corinthian style, supporting arches, and forming numerous aisles with their ranges. . .

'. . . At present, some Jews and Armenians have established a silk manufactory here. Spinning-wheels and winders buzz beneath the arches of Constantine, and the noise of looms imitates the rippling of the waters which have disappeared. There reigns in this subterranean region – half lighted and half buried in profound shadow – an icy coldness, which chills the visitor; and it is with a lively sensation of pleasure, that he remounts, from the depths of this gulf, into the warm glow of the sunshine; pitying, sincerely, the poor work-people, patiently pursuing their tasks, like gnomes or kobolds, in their cold and dreary cavern.'[18]

Gautier's main concern, appropriate to the literary convention of realism, is with exteriors, either of articles or social customs. Like many previous and later travellers, the overt differences between East and West in small daily events like eating, entertaining, travelling, dressing, assume great importance for him. Thus he presents detailed descriptions of decorated rooms, complete with carpets and furniture, although his interest in carpets does not extend into the scientific.

'The apartment in which the Pasha's wife received her guest, was both rich and elegant, . . . The floor was covered by a superb Smyrna carpet, upon which the heaviest foot would fall noiselessly; the ceiling was decorated with coloured and gilded arabesques; a long divan, of yellow and blue satin, ran along two entire sides of the room, and another very low divan stood between two windows, from which was seen a splendid view of the Bosphorus in full perspective.'[19]

Also present are fascinating glimpses of encounters in the city with people from all walks of life and the symbols of their lifestyles.

'This boat carried a Pasha, bound for Gallipolis, at the mouth of the Sea of Marmora. . .

'. . . A numerous suite surrounded him – officers, secretaries, pipe-bearers, and other domestic officers, without counting *cawas* and domestics. All these people unfolded carpets, or unrolled mattresses, and seated themselves upon them with the exception of some few, better bred, who sat down upon the benches, and consoled themselves for taking that unnatural position, by holding one of their feet in one of their hands, as a

comfort and an occupation.

'Their luggage was curious. There were narghiles, enclosed in red morocco cases; packets of pipe-stems, of cherry or jasmin; baskets, covered with richly-gilded leather, to do duty as portmanteaus; rolls of Persian carpet, and piles of cushions and footstools.'[20]

A contrasting though nevertheless very realistic and matter-of-fact observation was given twenty or so years earlier by the Prussian von Moltke. Since his biography is so well known, one bears in mind always that his view is that of an ambitious army officer and thus much to do with power relationships and practical action. However, he was in his leisure able to reflect on lifestyles in a manner which neither possesses English snobbery nor the overriding French concern with style and the exotic. It is interesting to note his view of the Sultan and the considerable European influence, especially French, which had been exerted upon him. It also goes to prove that not all carpets were part of a one-way traffic.

'[Audience with the Grand Seigneur 21.1.1837] . . . After a short respite we entered the living quarters. Since a certain degree of formality is necessary, chairs were set for us on the low flight of steps which was covered with fine carpets. After a few minutes we were summoned and Wassaf-Effendi immediately took off his sword; I was in civilian clothes. The rooms through which we walked are neither large nor very splendid. . .

'After a carpet had been drawn back from a side door,[21] we saw the Grand Seigneur in an armchair. I made three deep bows according to usual practice and then retreated to the door. His Imperial Majesty was wearing the red cap, the 'fez', and a broad violet-coloured coat, or rather a cloak, which concealed his whole figure and which was clasped with a diamond brooch. The Sultan was smoking a jasmine-stemmed pipe, the amber point set with beautiful jewels. His chair stood next to the long divan which is always placed here beneath the windows. By glancing to his left His Majesty was able to survey the most beautiful part of his empire, the capital, the fleet, the sea and the Asiatic mountains. On the right of the Grand Seigneur . . . stood six or seven of his court officials in profound silence . . . A fine French carpet covered the floor and in the middle of the room a coal-fire glowed in a splendid brass "mangal" [brazier].'[22]

The French carpet may have been an example of a Hereke work copying the French style. Certainly later, Hereke was able to direct its immense skill to using the designs of other traditions.

By the end of the century travellers had become much more interested in the lifestyles of Eastern countries and class divisions were increasingly broken, at least as far as the descriptions go. Some travellers, like Curzon, were interested in the total economic and political fabric with a view to how this might affect Western plans and overall supremacy, thus providing us with details on trade and industry, including carpet production.

'In some places, particularly at Kerman, the manufacture is pursued under very unhealthy conditions, the artisans being obliged to work underground in order to escape the dryness of the outer air, while the elasticity of the threads is preserved by moisture from vessels filled with water.'[23]

Others were humanely interested, as Curzon may well have been, in the actual working conditions which prevailed and in all aspects of the East's culture, wanting to participate rather than control or change. One such traveller was E G Browne, who as a scholar of Persian, a future Cambridge professor and possibly the greatest modern student of Persian literature, was very open to contact with ordinary people as well as the upper class. His sympathetic description of work in a Kirman shawl manufactory could equally well reflect production conditions within a carpet manufactory and serves to remind us of the hardship which the manufacturers were forced to undergo and which many people in the West did not, and probably still do not, appreciate.

'Saturday, 8th June, 28th Ramazan [1888] – In the morning I visited one of the shawl-manufactories of Kirmán in company with Rustam, Ná'ib Ḥasan, and Mírzá Yúsuf of Tabríz. Our way lay through the street leading to the Mosque Gate, which, by reason of the Saturday market (*Bázár-i-Shanba*), was thronged with people. The shawl-manufactory consisted of one large vaulted room containing eleven looms, two or three of which were standing idle. At each loom sat three workers, one skilled workman in the middle, and on either side of him a *shágird* or apprentice, whom he was expected to instruct and supervise. There were in all twenty-five apprentices, ranging in years from children of six and seven to men of mature age. Their wages, as I learned, begin at ten *túmáns* (about £3) a year, and increase gradually to twenty-four or twenty-five *túmáns* (about £7. 10s.). In summer they work from sunrise to sunset, and in winter they continue their work by candle-light till three hours after sunset. They have a half-holiday on Friday (from mid-day onwards), thirteen days' holiday at the *Nawrúz*, and one or two

days more on the great annual festivals, while for food they get nothing as a rule but dry bread. Poor little Kirmánís! They must toil thus, deprived of good air and sunlight, and debarred from the recreations and amusements which should brighten their childhood, that some grandee may bedeck himself with those sumptuous shawls, which, beautiful as they are, will evermore seem to me to be dyed with the blood of the innocents!'[24]

The consumer end of this production is represented by the testimony of Ella Sykes, who as companion to her brother in a diplomatic posting, had the opportunity to view the conditions of middle and upper classes alike. She shows particular interest in the carpets of Kirman, where she spent much of her time, although her interpretation of the images they carry may be somewhat askew. One thing to be noted is the price of a quality carpet!

'The Kerman carpets are of wonderfully fine texture, having the pattern clearly indicated on the reverse side, and are coloured with exquisite vegetable dyes. Like most Oriental carpets, they became handsomer after years of use, their colours blending into a mellow richness and subdued brightness. As a rule they are only made in small sizes, unless specially ordered, and are by no means cheap. We paid £8 for several of our carpets, not much larger than rugs, that being the cost price in Kerman. Birds, beasts, and even human figures are introduced into these carpets, and as this is entirely contrary to the tenets of Mohammedanism, it shows that the Kerman patterns are of great antiquity, and are prior to the Arab invasion of Persia.'[25]

Browne for his part gives us marvellous composite images of many aspects of Eastern life. The activities he indulged in during his extensive travels show how commonplace the use of the carpet was in the East and how it often designated the use of rooms or living areas where furniture or decoration would have done so in the West. It's the wonderful portability of the carpet which fits in so well with the itinerant Eastern concept of the home and comfort.

'There is, of course, no post-house at Mihr-ábád, nor, so far as I know, a caravansaray; but I was far from regretting this, as I obtained a much more delightful resting-place in a beautiful rose-garden near the gate of the village. . . In a sort of alcove in the high mud wall a carpet was spread for me, and here I esconced myself, Ḥájí Ṣafar taking up his position under the opposite wall. Tea was soon prepared, and while I was drinking it the gardener brought me two great handfuls of loose rose-leaves – a pretty custom, common in this more eastern part of Persia.'[26]

The vital thread between production and sale, the thread which linked trade, was the caravan. This method of transportation remained of paramount importance for carpets. Browne gives us a vivid portrayal of one such caravan on the move, describing the kinds of landscape he encountered, the climate and the Eastern atmosphere. All details which may well have had such an important effect on rug colour, images and design.

'After supper I lay gazing at the starry sky till sleep overcame me. About midnight Hájí Ṣafar awoke me, and soon afterwards we started at a good pace (for these caravans of donkeys travel faster than ordinary caravans) on the long desert stage which was to bring us to Cháh-Begí, the first habitable spot on the Yezd side of the desolate plain. Bare and hideous as this desert is by day, seen in the silver moonlight it had a strange weird beauty, which produced on me a deep impression. The salt-pools and salt-patches gleamed like snow on every side; the clear desert air was laden with a pungent briny smell like a sea-breeze; and over the sharply-defined hills of Yezd, towards which we were now directly advancing, hung the great silvery moon to the right, and the "Seven Brothers" (haft birádarán), or Great Bear, to the left. I kept in advance of the caravan, and watched with a keen pleasure the stars "beginning to faint on a bed of daffodil sky", till first the "caravan-killer" (káraván- or chárvádár-kush) and then the morning star dissolved in the rosy flush which crept upwards from behind the eastern mountains, and suddenly, like a ball of fire, the sun leaped up over their serrated summits, scattering the illusions of the night, and bringing into view chains and ridges of low hills which had hitherto seemed to form part of the main mass. . .'[27]

Browne's especial interest in philosophy and the discussions attendant on this also produce an interesting picture of Eastern philosophy and a view of Westerners through Eastern eyes, highlighting the different patterns of thought and the conception of self and society. The advantage he had over many travellers was his knowledge of Eastern culture, language and history. This development of interest in anthropological and psychological concerns is also apparent in other travellers. Ella Sykes, like Lady Wortley Montagu two centuries earlier, was able to give a view of the woman's half of society as manifested both in lower and upper class circles. She did not escape middle class prejudices,

but, mostly by means of her servants, was able to look beyond those prejudices to the lives of ordinary people.[28]

Also, like Montagu before her, she testifies to the continuing tradition of leisure centring round the garden and its relationship with the carpet. Browne's caravan may have travelled at night to avoid the heat of the climate, but during the day coolness was found and leisure most frequently enjoyed where vegetation and thus water were prevalent.

'Sometimes we would go to a mountain village, set in the midst of a stony desert, its fertilising stream making it an oasis in the dreary desolation all around. Tea would be spread on a carpet, perhaps in a garden of pomegranates, the scarlet blossoms glowing like flames out of the gloom of the surrounding trees, and the proprietor of the place would bring us a great tray of mulberries, apricots, and the much-esteemed short, fat cucumbers.'[29]

The importance to the Persians of the concept of the garden and its consequent reflection in rug patterns is something which is strongly conveyed by her descriptions. Rugs as physical objects and not simply as metaphorical reflections were an intrinsic part of the same idea.

Since the Renaissance at least, possibly in response to Eastern influence, gardens had been important concepts of order and enjoyment in the West, amid the continuing metaphorical resonance of The Garden of Eden. Likewise the paradisal implications of the garden were key elements in Eastern philosophical and religious thought, as Ella Sykes demonstrates:

'One afternoon we all rode to the garden made by Fath Ali Shah, in the little village of Fin, about four miles to the west of Kashan. This "Paradise" was laid out in avenues of big cypresses, these and poplars being the favourite trees of Persia; and at their feet channels of warm water ran over blue and green tiles. The large tanks which fed these ducts swarmed with small fish, and here and there were fine archways frescoed with the exploits of Fath Ali Shah.'[30]

Browne also gives an indication of the garden's importance to the East in its culture, philosophy and symbolism.

'The Persians take the greatest delight in their gardens, and show more pride in exhibiting them to the stranger than in pointing out to him their finest buildings. Yet to one accustomed to the gardens of the

West they appear, as a rule, nothing very wonderful. They generally consist of a square enclosure surrounded by a mud wall, planted with rows of poplar trees in long straight avenues, and intersected with little streams of water. The total absence of grass seems their greatest defect in the eyes of a European, but apart from this they do not, as a rule, contain a great variety of flowers, and, except in the spring, present a very bare appearance. But in the eyes of the Persian, accustomed to the naked stony plains which constitute so large a portion of his country, they appear as veritable gardens of Eden, and he will never be happier than when seated under the shade of a poplar by the side of the stream, sipping his tea and smoking his *kalyán*[31]

As Browne notes, it is not surprising that the garden holds such fascination for the East when much of the country is so desolate. Similarly, the natural rhythms of the year are seen to hold enormous importance in Eastern minds, especially the coming of spring which amidst barren surroundings provides such welcome relief and confirmation of God's bounty, as rug patterns with their abundance of natural and stylised blossom and growth demonstrate. Ella Sykes also echoes this sentiment:

'Although it was a cold and dreary morning when we left Kuhpah, yet we could see that spring had come even to these desolate regions. Clumps of mauve crocuses were blossoming among the thorns, many of which were bursting into bud and leaf; a most unpromising-looking shrub was a mass of pink flowers resembling "London pride"; . . . As my brother quoted to me from the "Gulistan" of Sadi: "Not only the nightingale in the rose-bushes sings his hymn of praise, but every thorn is itself a voice of adoration to the Deity."'[32]

NOTES

1 Marlowe, C, *The Jew of Malta*, c.1592, I, i, 21-23, 25-28.
2 Rowse, A L, *Christopher Marlowe: A Biography*, London, 1964, pp. 19-20.
3 Marlowe, C, *Tamburlaine*, c.1587, pt. 2, I, iii, 40-44.
4 See *The Eastern Carpet in the Western World*.
5 Marlowe, C, *The Jew of Malta*, IV, ii, 106-111.
6 Halsband, R, ed., *The Complete Letters of Lady Mary Wortley Montagu, 1708-1720*, Oxford, 1965.
7 Translated into French by Antoine Galland in the early 18th century.
8 Keats, J, *The Eve of St. Agnes*, 1819, ll. 268-270.
9 Byron, Lord George, *Don Juan*, 1819-1824, Canto III, LXVII.
10 See, for example, Keats's poem, *The Castle Builder*, ll. 25-30, in which he satirises the popular interior decoration of the day, including the use of Turkish floor coverings.
11 Keats, J, *The Cap and Bells, or the Jealousies*, c.1819, ll. 343-347.
12 Beckford, F, *Vathek*, 1782 – the story of the Caliph Vathek who becomes the servant of the fallen angel, Iblis, but eventually realises the vanity of earthly possessions. Beckford's *Recollections of the Monasteries of Alcobaca and Batalha*, 1835, exemplified the North European attraction for buildings in the Iberian Peninsula which showed a marked Eastern influence.
13 Compare the effect on Washington Irving whose *Legends of the Alhambra*, 1832, proceeded from his duties with the American Legation in Spain.
14 Halsband, op. cit., pp. 313-314.
15 Halsband, op. cit., pp. 342-343.
16 Halsband, op. cit., p. 331.
17 See *The Roving Englishman in Turkey* (1855), London, 1855, and the Earl of Carlisle, *Diary in Turkish and Greek Waters*, London, 1854, especially pp. 44-46.
18 Gautier, op. cit., pp. 317-318.
19 Gautier, op. cit., p. 203.
20 Gautier, op. cit., pp. 73-74.
21 Evidently a 'portière'.
22 Moltke, Helmut von, *Briefe aus der Türkei, 1835-1839*, Köln, 1968, pp. 128-129.
23 Curzon, op. cit., vol. 2, pp. 523-524.
24 Browne, op. cit., pp. 482-483.
25 Sykes, E, *Through Persia on a Side-Saddle*, London, 1901, p. 100.
26 Browne, op. cit., pp. 382-383.
27 Browne, op. cit., pp. 386-387.
28 Sykes, op. cit.: see especially pp. 82-85 where she describes the attitudes and behaviour of her servants.
29 Sykes, op. cit., p. 114.
30 Sykes, op. cit., p. 47.
31 Browne, op. cit., p. 95.
32 Sykes, op. cit., p. 52.

BIBLIOGRAPHY

Albarn, K, Miall Smith, J, Steele, S, and Walker, D, *The Language of Pattern*, London, 1974.

Allen, F L, *The Great Pierpont Morgan*, New York, 1949.

Allott, M, ed., *The Poems of John Keats*, London, 1970.

Ardalan, N, and Bakhtiar, L, *The Sense of Unity*, Chicago and London, 1973.

Armstrong, H C, *Grey Wolf: Mustafa Kemal – An intimate study of a dictator*, London, 1932.

Beattie, M, *The Thyssen-Bornemisza Collection of Oriental Rugs*, Lugarno, 1972.
  Carpets of Central Persia, exhibition catalogue, London, 1976.
  'Hereke', *Hali*, 1981, vol. 4, no. 14.

Bennett, I, *Rugs and Carpets of the World*, London, reprinted 1985.

Bensoussan, P, 'The Masterweavers of Istanbul', *Hali*, 1985, no. 26.

Black, D, ed., *World Rugs and Carpets*, London, 1985.

Bode, W von, and Kühnel, E, *Antique Rugs from the Near East*, trans. C G Ellis, London, 1970.

Bronimann, A, *Splendeur du Tapis d'Orient*, Paris, 1974.

Brookes, J, *Gardens of Paradise*, London, 1987.

Browne, E G, *A Year Among the Persians*, London, 1983, new ed.

Byron, Lord George, *Poetical Works*, ed. F Page, London, 1970.

Cambridge History of Islam, Cambridge, 1970, vol. 1.

Cambridge History of Iran, Cambridge, 1986, vol. 6.

Cammann, S, 'Symbolic Meanings in Oriental Rug Patterns – Pt 1', *Textile Museum Journal*, 111/3, December 1972.
  'The Interplay of Art, Literature, and Religion in Ṣafavid Symbolism', *JRAS*, 1978, no. 2.

Carlisle, Earl of, *Diary in Turkish and Greek Waters*, London, 1854.

Çelik, Z, *The Remaking of Istanbul*, Seattle and London, 1986.

Critchlow, K, *Islamic Patterns*, London, 1976.

Curzon, G, *Persia and the Persian Question*, London, 1892, 2 vols.

Darby, M, *The Islamic Perspective*, London, 1983.

Denny, W B, 'The Origin of the Designs of Ottoman Court Carpets', *Hali*, 1979, vol. 2, no. 1.

Dimand, M S, and Mailey, J, *Oriental Rugs in The Metropolitan Museum of Art*, New York, 1973.

The Eastern Carpet in the Western World, exhibition catalogue, Hayward Gallery, London, 1983.

Edwards, C, *The Persian Carpet*, London, 1967.

The Encyclopaedia of Islam, second edition, articles 'Akhī', 'Ḥarīr', 'Ḥisba', 'Muḥtasib' and 'Ṣinf'.

Erdmann, K, *Oriental Carpets*, London, 1960.
  Seven Hundred Years of Oriental Carpets, Berkeley, 1970.

Fairclough, P, ed., *Three Gothic Novels*, Harmondsworth, 1968.

Falk, S J, *Qajar Paintings*, London, 1972.

Firdawsī, *The Epic of the Kings*, trans. R Levy, London, 1967.

Fitzgerald, E, *Rubáiyát of Omar Khayyám*, London, 1944.

Focillon, H, *The Art of the West – Romanesque*, Oxford, 1980, revised ed.

Franses, J, *European and Oriental Rugs*, London, 1970.

Gaunt, W, *The Impressionists*, London, 1970.

Gautier, T, *Constantinople of To-day*, trans. R Howe Gould, London, 1854.

Gombrich, E H, 'Aims and Limits of Iconology', *Symbolic Images*, London, 1972.

Goodwin, G, *A History of Ottoman Architecture*, London, 1971.
  Ottoman Turkey, London, 1977.

Gray, B, ed., *The Arts of the Book in Central Asia*, London, 1979.

Haldane, D, *Islamic Bookbindings*, London, 1983.

Halsband, R, ed., *The Complete Letters of Lady Mary Wortley Montagu, 1708-1720*, Oxford, 1965.

Hamilton, R W, *Khirbat al-Mafjar*, Oxford, 1959.

Hanaway, W L, Jr., 'Paradise on Earth: the Terrestrial Garden in Persian Literature', *The Islamic Garden*, Dumbarton Oaks, 1976.

Harrow, L, *Oriental Rugs in Private Collections*, London, 1982.
  The Bellairs Collection, London, 1986.
  From the Lands of Sultan and Shah, London, 1987.

Ḥudūd al-'Ālam, trans. V Minorsky, London, 1970, 2nd ed.

Hutt, A, and Harrow, L, *Iran 1*, London, 1977.
  Iran 2, London, 1978.

Issawi, C, *The Economic History of Iran*, Chicago and London, 1971.

Kendrick, A F, Pope, A U, and Thomson, W G, *The Emperor's Carpet and Two Others*, London, 1928.

Kühnel, E, *Islamic Arts*, trans. K Watson, London, 1970.

Lambton, A K S, *Qajar Persia*, London, 1987.

Lane, A, *A Guide to the Collection of Tiles*, London, 1960.

Lane, E, *The Manners and Customs of the Modern Egyptians*, London, 1908 (rep. 1966).

Lewis, B, *The Emergence of Modern Turkey*, London, 1981, 2nd ed.

Lewis, R, *Everyday Life in the Ottoman Empire*, London, 1971.

MacFarlane, C, *Turkey and its Destiny*, London, 1850, 2 vols.

der Manuelian, L, and Eiland, M L, *Weavers, Merchants and Kings*, Fort Worth, 1984.

Miller, D, *Zareh Penyamine*, catalogue, London, n.d.

Mills, J, 'Early Animal Carpets in Western Paintings – A Review', *Hali*, 1978, vol. 1, no. 3.
  'Small Pattern Holbein Carpets in Western Paintings', *Hali*, 1978, vol. 1, no. 4.
  '"Lotto" Carpets in Western Paintings', *Hali*, 1981, vol. 3, no. 4.
  'East Mediterranean Carpets in Western Paintings', *Hali*, 1981, vol. 4, no. 1.

Moltke, Helmut von, *Briefe aus der Türkei, 1835-1839*, Köln, 1968.

Morier, J, *The Adventures of Hajji Baba of Ispahan*, London, 1824 (rep. 1914).

Moynihan, E B, *Paradise as a Garden*, New York, 1979.

Muir, W, *The Caliphate, its Rise, Decline and Fall*, Beirut, rep. 1963.

Nasr, S H, *Introduction to Islamic Cosmological Doctrines*, London, 1976.
  The Encounter of Man and Nature, the Spiritual Crisis of Modern Man, London, 1968.

der Nersessian, S, *The Armenians*, London, 1969.

Paintings from the Muslim Courts of India, exhibition catalogue, British Museum, London, 1976.

Papazian, K Z, *Merchants from Ararat*, New York, 1979.

Penzer, N M, *The Harēm*, London, 1936.

Petsopoulos, Y, *Tulips, Arabesques and Turbans*, London, 1982.

Pope, A U, *A Survey of Persian Art*, Oxford, 1939, and Tokyo, 1967.

The Roving Englishman in Turkey (1855), London, 1855.

Rowse, A L, *Christopher Marlowe: A Biography*, London, 1964.

El-Said, I, and Parman, A, *Geometric Concepts in Islamic Art*, London, 1976.

Sakisian, A, *Pages d'art arménien*, Paris, 1940.

Schimmel, A, 'The Celestial Garden in Islam', *The Islamic Garden*, Dumbarton Oaks, 1976.

Schlamminger, K, and Wilson, P L, *Persische Bildteppiche*, Munich, 1980.

Serjeant, R B, *Islamic Textiles*, Beirut, 1972.

Steane, J B, ed., *Christopher Marlowe, The Complete Plays*, London, 1969.

Storr, A, *Jung*, London, 1973.

Strange, G Le, *Lands of the Eastern Caliphate*, London, 1905.

Sykes, E, *Through Persia on a Side-Saddle*, London, 1901.

Sykes, P, *A History of Persia*, London, 1930, vol. ii.

Talbot Rice, T, *The Saljuqs*, London, 1961.

Tebbel, J, *The Life and Good Times of William Randolph Hearst*, London, 1953.
  The Inheritors, New York, 1962.

Topalian, M F, 'Rug Merchants in America', *Hali*, June, 1982, no. 16.

Topukapu Kyuden Hakubutsukan, Tokyo, 1980.

Trenkwald, H, and Sarre, F, *Old Oriental Carpets*, Vienna and Leipzig, 1926, vol. I, and 1929, vol. II.

Waardenburg, J, 'Symbolic Aspects of Myth', *Myth, Symbol and Reality*, ed. A M Olson, Notre Dame (Ind), 1980.

Widener, P A B, *Without Drums*, New York, 1940.

Wilber, D N, 'Heriz Rugs', *Hali*, 1984, vol. 6, no. 21.

Wulff, H, *Traditional Crafts of Persia*, Cambridge (Mass.), 1966.